Macmillan
ENCYCLOPEDIA OF SCIENCE

7

The Environment
Ecology, Pollution, and Agriculture

Clint Twist

Macmillan Publishing Company
New York

Maxwell Macmillan International Publishing Group
New York   Oxford   Singapore   Sydney

Published by:
Macmillan Publishing Company
A Division of Macmillan, Inc.
866 Third Avenue, New York, NY 10022

Collier Macmillan Canada, Inc.
1200 Eglinton Avenue East, Suite 200
Don Mills, Ontario M3C 3N1

Planned and produced by Andromeda Oxford Ltd.

Copyright © 1991 Andromeda Oxford Ltd.
Macmillan edition copyright © 1991 Macmillan Publishing Company

Library of Congress Cataloging-in-Publication Data

Macmillan encyclopedia of science.
          p.   cm.
     Includes bibliographical references and index.
     Summary: An encyclopedia of science and technology, covering such areas as the Earth, the ocean, plants and animals, medicine, agriculture, manufacturing, and transportation.
     ISBN 0-02-941346-X (set)
     1. Science–Encyclopedias, Juvenile.   2. Engineering–Encyclopedias, Juvenile.   3. Technology–Encyclopedias, Juvenile.
     [1. Science–Encyclopedias.   2. Technology–Encyclopedias.]
     I. Macmillan Publishing Company   90-19940
     Q121.M27   1991   CIP
     503 – dc20   AC

Volumes of the *Macmillan Encyclopedia of Science*
 1 *Matter and Energy* ISBN 0-02-941141-6
 2 *The Heavens* ISBN 0-02-941142-4
 3 *The Earth* ISBN 0-02-941143-2
 4 *Life on Earth* ISBN 0-02-941144-0
 5 *Plants and Animals* ISBN 0-02-941145-9
 6 *Body and Health* ISBN 0-02-941146-7
 7 *The Environment* ISBN 0-02-941147-5
 8 *Industry* ISBN 0-02-941341-9
 9 *Fuel and Power* ISBN 0-02-941342-7
10 *Transportation* ISBN 0-02-941343-5
11 *Communication* ISBN 0-02-941344-3
12 *Tools and Tomorrow* ISBN 0-02-941345-1

Printed in the United States of America

Introduction

Living things exist in a complex network of relations with each other and their environment. This volume explores such relations. It focuses particularly on the impact of human activities on the balance of nature and surveys the plants and animals used in agriculture. Much information here is presented in photographs, drawings, and diagrams. They are well worth your attention.

To learn about a specific topic, start by consulting the Index at the end of the book. You can find all the references in the encyclopedia to the topic by turning to the final Index, covering all 12 volumes, located in Volume 12.

If you come across an unfamiliar word while using this book, the Glossary may be of help. A list of key abbreviations can be found on page 87. If you want to learn more about the subjects covered in the book, look at the Further Reading section.

Scientists tend to express measurements in units belonging to the "International System," which incorporates metric units. This encyclopedia accordingly uses metric units (with American equivalents also given in the main text). More information on units of measurement is on page 86.

Contents

Part One

Ecology and Pollution

Human beings live on a very crowded planet; we share the Earth with about 30 million other species. The study of life in its natural environment is called ecology. Ecologists study the relationships between species, and their behavior.

Human feeding, directly or indirectly, has been responsible for centuries of accumulated damage to the environment. Whole landscapes have been transformed by the axe and the plow, and much wildlife has been hunted out of existence.

For over 300 years, we have been recording extinctions: the disappearance of entire species. Thousands of species are now endangered.

Human beings also bear responsibility for polluting the environment with chemicals. Some are deadly poisons, some may alter the climate of the whole planet; all of them in some way threaten the future of the Earth.

◀ Manhattan, New York, by night. One of the most crowded places on Earth, the city shows how successful humans have been in colonizing the planet. But how costly is our success?

Nature in balance

▶ City schoolchildren at a pond in Essex, England. Environmental education is becoming more common in many countries. Concern is growing about the many threats to wildlife and the balance of nature posed by the growth of industry and human populations. Young people are especially keen to play their part in restoring the natural balance.

No living organism exists in complete isolation from others. Plants and animals that live in a particular place share the same air, the same rocks, and the same neighbors. They live together, and they live in harmony. Some feed on others, but the larger picture is one of overall balance.

Scientific studies have shown that this balance is achieved through an extremely complex network of relationships between different species. One of the most important relationships is that between plants and animals. Without plants, animal life would be impossible.

Habitats and ecosystems

Levels of study in ecology

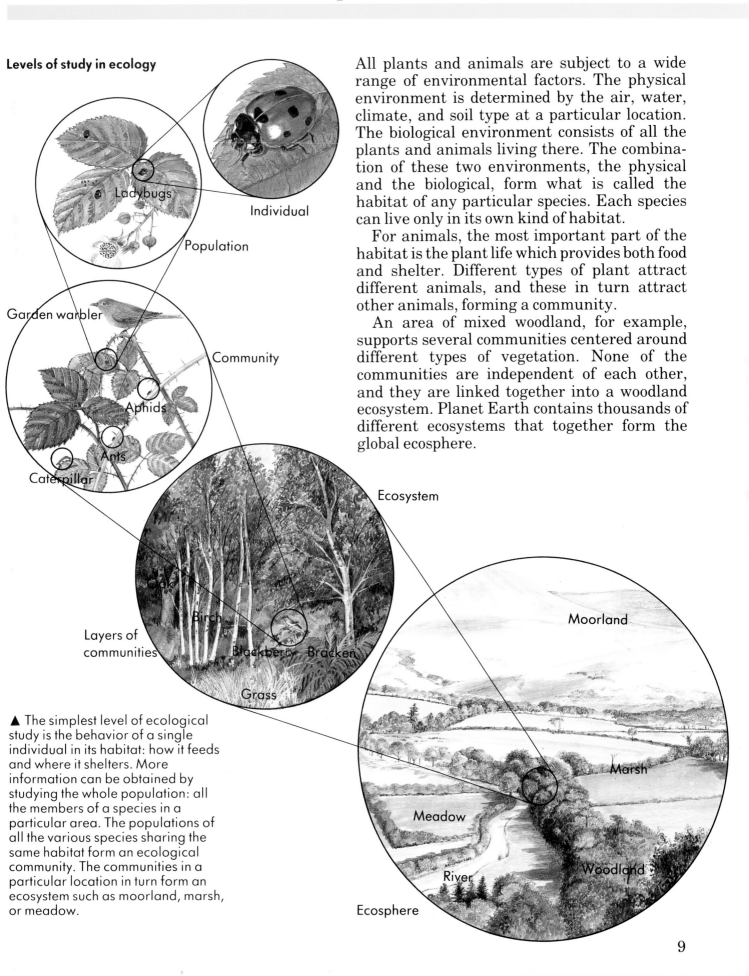

Individual

Population

Ladybugs

Garden warbler

Community

Aphids

Ants

Caterpillar

Layers of communities

Birch

Blackberry

Bracken

Grass

Ecosystem

Moorland

Marsh

Meadow

River

Woodland

Ecosphere

All plants and animals are subject to a wide range of environmental factors. The physical environment is determined by the air, water, climate, and soil type at a particular location. The biological environment consists of all the plants and animals living there. The combination of these two environments, the physical and the biological, form what is called the habitat of any particular species. Each species can live only in its own kind of habitat.

For animals, the most important part of the habitat is the plant life which provides both food and shelter. Different types of plant attract different animals, and these in turn attract other animals, forming a community.

An area of mixed woodland, for example, supports several communities centered around different types of vegetation. None of the communities are independent of each other, and they are linked together into a woodland ecosystem. Planet Earth contains thousands of different ecosystems that together form the global ecosphere.

▲ The simplest level of ecological study is the behavior of a single individual in its habitat: how it feeds and where it shelters. More information can be obtained by studying the whole population: all the members of a species in a particular area. The populations of all the various species sharing the same habitat form an ecological community. The communities in a particular location in turn form an ecosystem such as moorland, marsh, or meadow.

9

Themes in ecology

Ecology is the study of how species react to other species. By studying the relationships and interactions between species in a community, ecologists can learn how a balance is maintained in nature. The feeding behavior of animals is one of the most important interactions. Plants can meet their own needs from sunlight, carbon dioxide, water, and nutrients in the soil. Animals have to actively search for food, since they cannot make their own.

An area of woodland may support a population of millions of flying insects. These offer a rich source of food for airborne predators able to catch them in the air. This role is filled by certain birds and bats. A position within an ecosystem such as this is called a niche.

Animals may feed on the caterpillars of the same insects, but occupy a different niche. Similarly, birds and bats occupy different niches because the birds hunt by day and the bats by night. This separation of niches avoids unnecessary competition for food. In general, each potential niche tends to be occupied by only one or two different species. Any more would make an imbalance.

Feeding behavior is central to defining a niche, but other interactions are also very important to the ecosystem. Many animals are essential to plant reproduction. Insects fertilize flowers while feeding, and birds and mammals are used by plants to carry seeds great distances. Some interactions are extremely specific, and occur only between two species; others involve many species.

▲ The African bushveld elephant shrew specializes in eating termites, an abundant source of food. The behavior of any species is largely determined by its habitat.

◄ The giraffe occupies a very successful niche on the African plains. Its long neck enables it to feed on vegetation that is above other animals' heads.

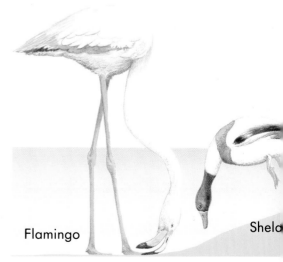

Flamingo   Shela

Succession

One year

Five years

25 years

When new land is created, or old land is cleared, a new community is born. The first living colonists will be plants suited to the open conditions. Plants are vital in forming and shaping a habitat. Their roots hold the soil together, and a mass of vegetation can moderate the effects of harsh climates. As the first community develops, it creates the shelter and shade necessary to nurture the next group of less hardy plants.

This progressive occupation of land is known as succession. Different types of vegetation follow distinctive patterns of succession. It may take hundreds of years for plants to turn these sand dunes into firm ground. After one year, grasses have already taken root. After five years, shrubs and small trees are established. After 25 years, the process is well under way, though far from complete.

Ecosystems do not suddenly come into existence; they are the result of many centuries of evolution. A community, on the other hand, can form during a much shorter period of time. Usually, the community will go through a series of stages before reaching its final form, which is known as a climax community. Whatever the ecosystem – prairie, tundra, woodland, or jungle – a climax community will regenerate itself indefinitely under natural conditions. If a small part is damaged, it soon builds up again.

The first inhabitants of a community, which are known as pioneer species, arrive as wind-borne seeds and flying insects. On coasts and islands they may also be washed up by the sea.

At first there are relatively few interactions. As the community develops, other species may displace the pioneers, only to be displaced themselves as succession continues. Climax communities usually contain a wide variety of plant or animal species, linked by a very complex network of interactions.

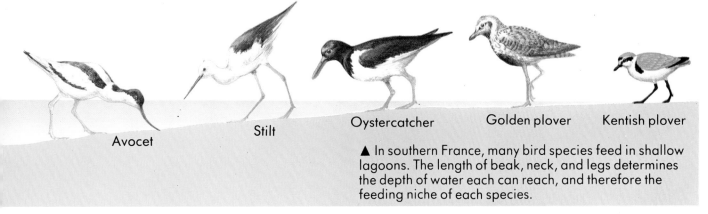

Avocet
Stilt
Oystercatcher
Golden plover
Kentish plover

▲ In southern France, many bird species feed in shallow lagoons. The length of beak, neck, and legs determines the depth of water each can reach, and therefore the feeding niche of each species.

Food webs

The ultimate source of food and energy for most living things is the Sun. By studying feeding habits, ecologists can trace the flow of energy through an ecosystem. The process of photosynthesis enables plants to manufacture their own food. They are called primary producers.

Animals that feed directly on plants (herbivores) are known as primary consumers. Animals that obtain their food from other animals (carnivores) are called secondary consumers. These different levels of feeding can be linked together into a food chain which always begins with a form of vegetation. The stages in the chain are often described as belonging to different trophic levels.

Food chains link together individual plant and animal species. The various food chains within an ecosystem can be combined to create a much more complex food web. At the summit of the food web are the top predators, whose food energy may have passed through as many as five different organisms. The final members in the food web are the decomposers. These are the bacteria and fungi that break down dead organic matter into its component parts and return the nutrients to the environment.

Food web in a temperate lake

- First trophic level (primary producers)
- Second trophic level (herbivores)
- Third trophic level
- Fourth trophic level
- Fifth trophic level
- Sixth trophic level

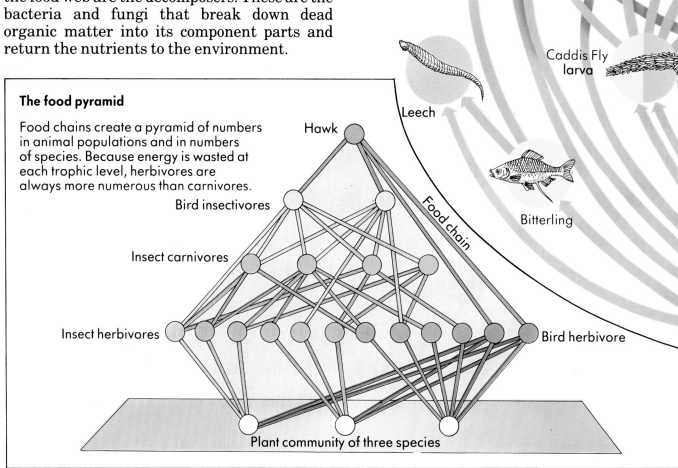

Frog/tadpole

Duck

Leech

Caddis Fly larva

Bitterling

Food chain

The food pyramid

Food chains create a pyramid of numbers in animal populations and in numbers of species. Because energy is wasted at each trophic level, herbivores are always more numerous than carnivores.

Hawk

Bird insectivores

Insect carnivores

Insect herbivores

Bird herbivore

Plant community of three species

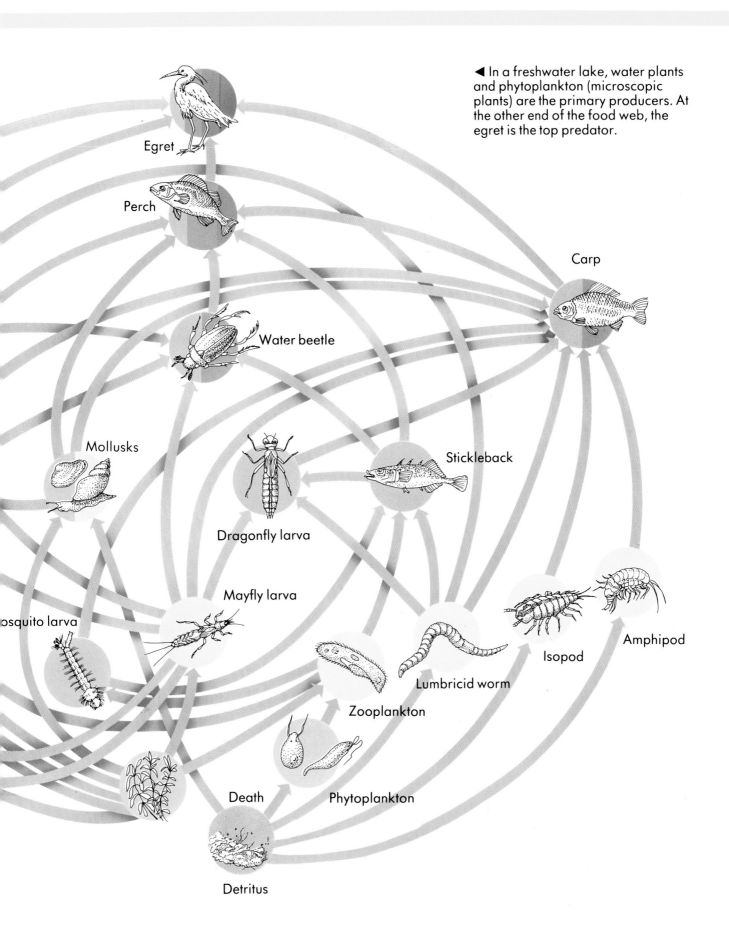

◄ In a freshwater lake, water plants and phytoplankton (microscopic plants) are the primary producers. At the other end of the food web, the egret is the top predator.

Egret

Perch

Carp

Water beetle

Mollusks

Stickleback

Dragonfly larva

Amphipod

Mayfly larva

Isopod

osquito larva

Lumbricid worm

Zooplankton

Death

Phytoplankton

Detritus

13

In the tropical rain forest

The tropical rain forests of South America, Africa, and Southeast Asia are among the most complex ecosystems that exist. The hot, wet conditions have encouraged the development of an incredible variety of species. More than half the species on Earth may be found in these forests. This diversity of life is one of the main characteristics of these ecosystems.

The unvarying climate ensures a year-round supply of fruit and flowers. The variety of habitats and food sources provides countless opportunities for primary consumers. These in turn create niches for carnivores. In general, populations tend to be small, with many species existing in self-contained "island" communities.

A layered environment
The rain forests form a multilayered, three-dimensional environment. At the top is the canopy, a mass of leaves over 30 m (100 ft.) above the ground. The middle layer, the understory, is fairly open, but is crisscrossed with creepers. The ground is largely free of vegetation, because little sunlight can penetrate through the dense overhead cover.

Animal life is concentrated in and around the canopy, attracted there by the limitless supplies of food. The understory forms a kind of internal road network. The uncluttered space allows rapid movement by birds and monkeys. The ground is largely left to insects and the forest's few large mammals.

Animal life plays a vital role in maintaining the forest. Many species carry pollen between flowers as they feed. The seeds of some trees will not germinate unless they have passed through the intestine of a particular species of monkey. Using monkeys to scatter seeds far and wide is just one of the ways the forest preserves its enormous variety of plant species.

▶ Examples of most kinds of animal live in the rain forest. Snakes, such as the boa constrictor (1), are generally found near the forest floor, although many are excellent tree climbers. Insects are found at all levels; the red stainer bugs (2) feed on fruit that has fallen to the ground. The coati, a small mammal (3), hunts lizards and insects, mainly on the ground. Fruit-eating bats (4) are widespread, and the howler monkey (5), is one of the largest mammals to inhabit the canopy. Its distinctive call can be heard echoing through the forest.

35 m

15 m

In the oceans

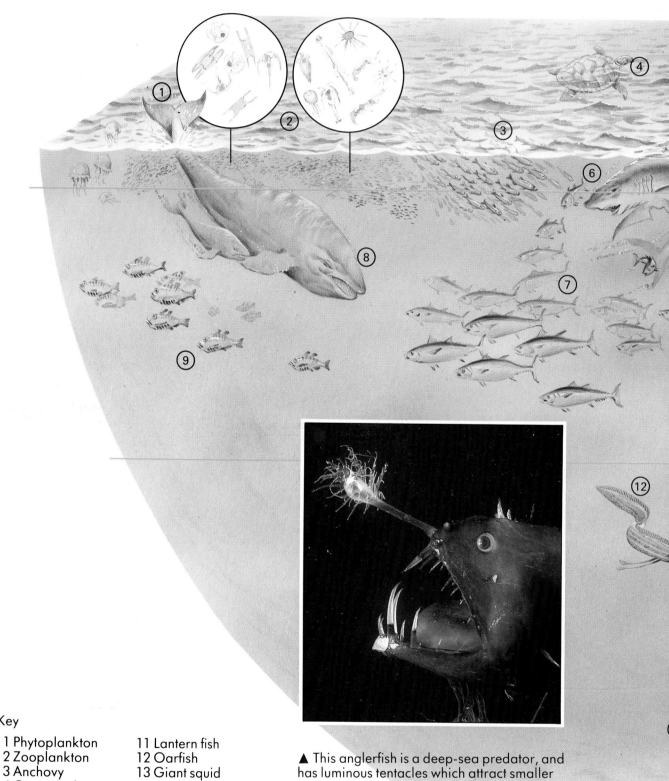

Key

1 Phytoplankton
2 Zooplankton
3 Anchovy
4 Green turtle
5 Dolphin
6 Shark
7 Bluefin tuna
8 Gray whale
9 Hatchetfish
10 Squid

11 Lantern fish
12 Oarfish
13 Giant squid
14 Deep-sea jellyfish
15 Skate
16 Brittle star
17 Deep-sea shrimp
18 Anglerfish
19 Tripod fish
20 Sea cucumber

▲ This anglerfish is a deep-sea predator, and has luminous tentacles which attract smaller fish to eat in the dark waters of the ocean bottom. Food resources are scarce in the murky depths, and so most species rely on the scanty amounts of detritus (dead organic matter) that drift down from the upper layers. The anglerfish is in danger of attracting enemies with its lure as well as its prey.

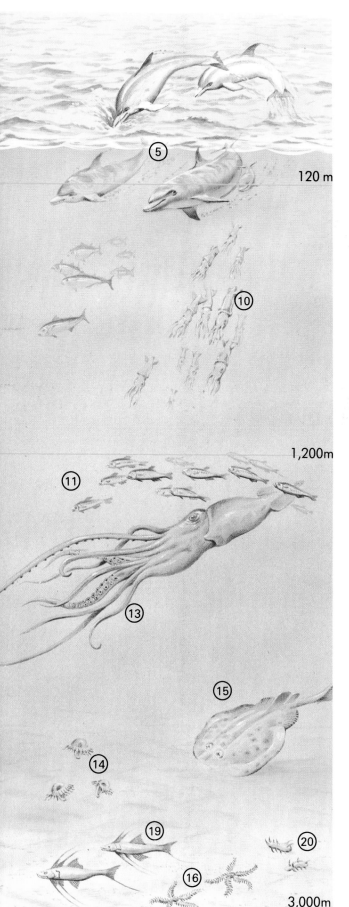

120 m

1,200m

3,000m

▲ The coral reef is a very rich habitat with thousands of species dependent on each other. At the bottom of the food web are the tiny plant plankton.

The oceans, which cover 70 percent of the Earth's surface, contain a number of distinct ecosystems. The most productive areas are coral reefs and shallow coastal waters, where every available surface teems with life.

The ecosystem of the deep ocean falls into distinct layers. Near the surface live the microscopic plankton that are the basis of the food web. Most of the familiar species of fish inhabit this layer, together with whales, dolphins, and other aquatic mammals. Below 1,000 m (3,000 ft.), life is much scarcer because plants cannot live in the permanent darkness. Fish in this layer tend to be much smaller, although carnivores like the giant squid can grow to great size. There are also giant worms.

Plankton is the basis of life in the oceans. There are two types: microscopic plants (phytoplankton) and tiny animals (zooplankton). At the other end of the ocean's food web are the predators such as the shark, which is one of the top predators.

17

Habitats at risk

Spot facts

● Up to 200,000 sq km (nearly 80,000 sq. mi.) of tropical rain forest are destroyed every year. If this continues, the rain forest could substantially disappear within the next 50 years.

● 11 million hectares (27 million acres) of crop-growing land are lost each year because of soil erosion. An additional 7 million hectares (17 million acres) of grassland are lost to the gradual process of desertification.

● Lake Volta in Ghana, West Africa, is the world's largest artificial lake. Formed by the Akosombo Dam, it now covers 8,500 sq km (3,300 sq. mi.) of drowned land.

Our own species, *Homo sapiens sapiens*, thrives on planet Earth. Human ingenuity has enabled our population to rise way beyond any natural limits, but only at a considerable cost to nature. Our method of food production, agriculture, is not a natural process. In one sense, we are the ultimate predators, because we consume entire habitats in the struggle to feed ourselves. Sometimes we succeed only in creating wasteland which cannot be used by wildlife or ourselves.

Mining, road building, and many other human activities also threaten the balance of nature. As a result, wildlife habitats around the world are now at risk. Only concerted action, by governments, organizations, and individuals, can save them.

► This lizard is one of the lucky ones being rescued by nature conservationists as its habitat is being destroyed. It lived in the area flooded by the new reservoir created by the Itaipu Dam at the Brazil-Paraguay border. There is frequently an outcry at the destruction of natural habitats during land development, but rarely can the work be halted to save them.

Nature and humankind

In 1960 the world's human population reached 3 billion; today it is over 5 billion and still rising. This increase in numbers places enormous pressure on the planet's resources, especially for food. Each night, one in seven human beings goes to sleep hungry. Until very recently, growing more food brought us into direct conflict with natural habitats. It meant cutting down more trees and clearing more land for the plow.

For centuries, agriculture has been transforming the landscape. We first started clearing the forests over 5,000 years ago to make room for flocks and herds. Agriculture brings us into direct conflict with nature. When farming, we are imposing our own food web, with human beings at the top, on natural ecosystems. Anything that threatens our food supplies threatens our lives. We compete with wildlife for space in which we need to grow food.

Food is not the only burden that human beings place on the environment. We are the only species with a completely unnatural lifestyle. Also, people need water, clothing, fuel, and shelter. Half the world's timber production is burned as firewood, and the cheapest methods of extracting minerals are usually the most destructive.

Physical space is also required because people have to live somewhere, and increasingly they are moving into the wild. Sometimes the movement is bold and dramatic, as when millions of settlers move to new homes on uncleared land. But in general, there has been a slow and steady invasion of natural habitats.

▼ The human population is increasing rapidly. Every hour, 8,000 people are born. Most of the increase is taking place in tropical countries where the climate makes large-scale agriculture extremely difficult.

Using the land

Natural threats

The environment and landscapes that we know today have appeared only recently in our planet's history. They are largely the result of dramatic changes in the Earth's climate.

Many of the basic landforms were sculpted by glaciers during the last Ice Age. About 30,000 years ago, huge sheets of ice covered much of Europe and North America, and areas of forest were very much smaller. The ice sheets began to retreat about 20,000 years ago. As they did, they uncovered huge areas of land, enabling the forests to increase in size. This process is still continuing, and in Alaska there are spruce trees growing where there were glaciers only 200 years ago.

Ice ages are not the only form of landscaping that is beyond human control. Earthquakes, volcanoes, violent storms, even meteorites from outer space can also change the shape of the world we inhabit.

World land use

Only 11 percent of the Earth's land surface is suitable for agriculture. The best farmland is in the Northern Hemisphere.

Farming the Earth's land surfaces
(figures in million hectares)

1,300   780   1,430

2,860

3,640

2,990

△ Agricultural
Cannot be farmed:
△ Arid
◩ Infertile
△ Thin soils
◆ Waterlogged
△ Permafrost

Virtually all the land that is suitable for agriculture is now farmed. In the poorer countries, many people have to grow food on second-rate land that cannot sustain long-term usage. Crops become poorer every year.

Increased standards of living in the richer countries have also created greater demand for nonessentials. The result is that natural habitats are disappearing all over the world.

The northern limits of agriculture are being extended by the introduction of hybrid crops that mature during short summers. Grain fields now extend into the coniferous forest zone.

The world's temperate grasslands have long since been transformed by livestock and the plow. In the United States, there are only a few hectares of untouched prairie, which are now carefully preserved.

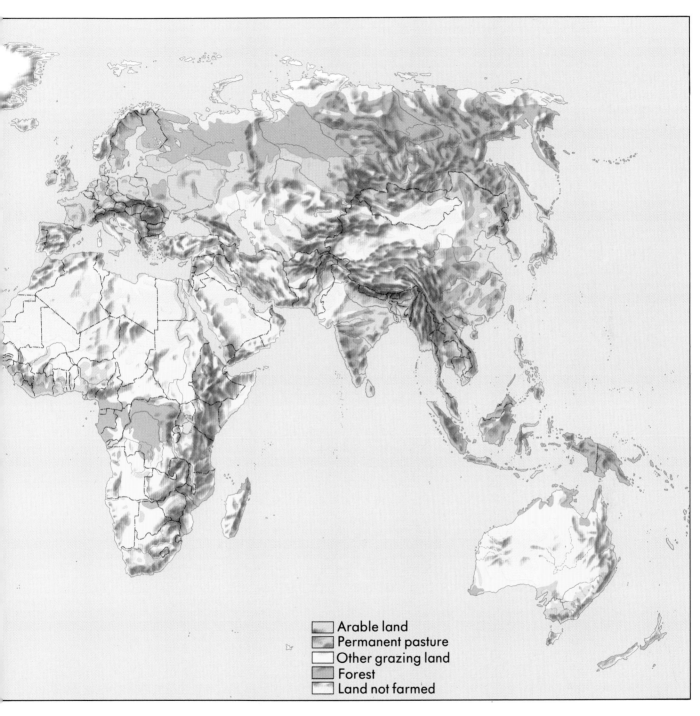

Arable land
Permanent pasture
Other grazing land
Forest
Land not farmed

In Africa, the Sahara Desert is slowly expanding southward. The fragile ecosystem at the fringe of the desert exists in precarious balance, with uncertain rainfall. Under the weight of human numbers, and overgrazing by the inhabitants' flocks, the ecosystem is breaking down completely. Without plants to hold the land together, there is no barrier to the approaching sand.

Machinery greatly multiplies the destructive effects of agriculture. In Europe and North America most of the natural forests were cut down long ago. A second wave of habitat destruction is now threatening those woods, hedgerows, and ponds which were unaffected by traditional farming methods. These refuges for wildlife are now being removed to create the huge fields required by modern machines.

Laying waste

The most dramatic example of habitat loss is the destruction of the tropical rain forests. The rain forests are disappearing at a rate of 1-2 percent per year. Ranching, plantations, mining, logging, and human settlement all demand their share of land. Within our lifetime, the rain forests may largely disappear. The greatest threat to them is agriculture. In South and Central America the rain forests are being burned down to create vast cattle ranches. Nearly all the meat produced is exported to be used in fast-food hamburger production.

This policy represents a very short-sighted use of resources which cannot be replaced. Heavy tropical rains will soon wash all the nutrients from the exposed soil. Experts predict that within 10 years, not even grass will grow where giant forest trees once stood. Once the grass dies, the soil itself will be washed away. Many scientists fear that the huge areas which have already been cleared will never regrow. The area could become a desert.

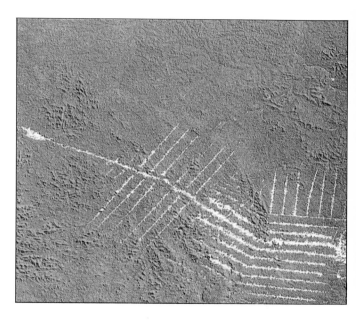

▲ The pattern of rain forest destruction in Brazil is clearly shown in this satellite image in which the vegetation shows up as red. Side roads branching off the main road give access to tree-cutting crews.

On a global scale, the rain forests represent huge masses of photosynthetic vegetation. They are responsible for recycling thousands of tons of carbon dioxide and oxygen every day. Without the rain forests, our atmosphere will gradually deteriorate.

Equally important is the rain forests' recycling of water. Over 75 percent of the rain that falls on the forests is returned to the atmosphere through evaporation and plant respiration. This water may travel halfway around the globe before it falls as rain again. Perhaps a quarter of the world's human population depends on this water from the rain forests.

Preserving the rain forests is not just a matter of saving some exotic species; it might be a case of saving life on Earth.

▶ Land in Upper Egypt poisoned by excess salt (salinization.) Irrigating the desert is one of the chief causes of salinization. As the irrigation water evaporates, it draws salt in the soil to the surface.

Unsuitable methods of agriculture can easily turn wildland into a wasteland. Natural grassland may include up to 40 different plant species. This varied mixture enables the ecosystem to flourish in regions of uncertain rainfall. There are enough drought-resistant species to survive dry spells. When people plow up the grassland to create fields of a single crop, they upset the careful balance of nature. If that crop dies because of drought, there is nothing to hold the soil together. It turns to dust, and may be blown or washed away.

This occurred on a large scale in the United States during the 1930s. Several years of low rainfall turned thousands of hectares of apparently good farmland into a "dust bowl." Logging operations are also tremendously destructive, and the damage is not confined to the valuable hardwood of the rain forests. For example, it takes over 400 hectares (1,000 acres) of medium-sized coniferous trees to make a single edition of a Sunday newspaper.

◀ A landscape transformed by overgrazing in Australia. Large herds of livestock are doubly damaging. They eat all the available vegetation, and also trample plants into the ground, preventing regrowth.

Engineering the landscape

Increased human population, concentrated in rapidly expanding cities, has greatly increased demand for fuel and minerals. The Earth contains a huge range of mineral treasures. Fuels such as coal, oil, and uranium, metals like aluminum and iron, and even the raw materials for concrete and glass, all have to be extracted from the ground.

Most of the mineral deposits that are readily accessible have already been exploited. The search for new supplies of fuel and metals is taking place in ever more remote areas, such as Siberia, Alaska, and the Amazon Basin.

A new discovery usually spells disaster for the surrounding habitat. Humans and machines move in to tame the wilderness, felling trees and tearing up the land.

In the case of gas and oil, the greatest damage is caused by the heavy equipment used to establish the field, and with time the ecosystem can usually recover. Long-term damage, however, may be caused by pipelines carrying hot crude oil across landscapes frozen into permafrost, especially if pipes crack.

▲ Open-pit china clay mine, Dartmoor, England. The local devastation caused by such mining operations is clearly apparent. In addition, mineral-laden dust may be carried great distances by the winds.

Open-pit and strip mining, employed where the mineral deposits lie just beneath the surface, is the most destructive form of exploitation. Coal, lignite, and many metal ores are commonly obtained in this manner. Huge, gaping holes are dug in the ground, disfiguring the landscape for many years.

Mining deep underground, for coal or metals, creates the opposite problem. The surrounding area becomes dotted with unsightly spoil heaps, artificial hills made of mud and rocks. In the long term, both forms of mining are equally destructive because bulky minerals require roads and railroads for shipping.

Roads help destroy natural habitats. They open up the land for exploitation. First the roadside area is cleared for firewood, then the land is used for recreation, and finally large areas are cleared for towns and cities.

Diverting water

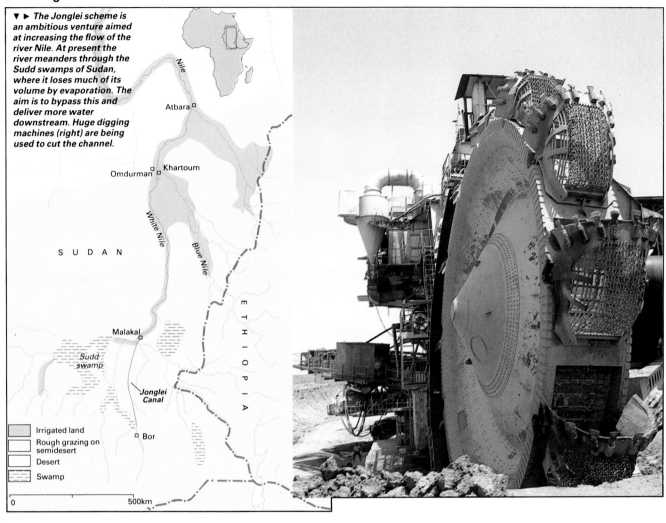

▼ ▶ The Jonglei scheme is an ambitious venture aimed at increasing the flow of the river Nile. At present the river meanders through the Sudd swamps of Sudan, where it loses much of its volume by evaporation. The aim is to bypass this and deliver more water downstream. Huge digging machines (right) are being used to cut the channel.

Nile
Atbara
Omdurman   Khartoum
White Nile
Blue Nile
S U D A N
E T H I O P I A
Malakal
Sudd swamp
Jonglei Canal
Bor

Irrigated land
Rough grazing on semidesert
Desert
Swamp

0   500km

▲ The Kariba Dam across the Zambesi River in East Africa is one of the world's largest, and was built to provide hydroelectric power.

▲ Throughout history, the most ambitious engineering projects have been concerned with water, or hydraulic engineering. There have been dams to hold back irrigation water, aqueducts to carry drinking water, and canals for transportation and drainage. Today, some of the biggest machines ever built are digging the Jonglei Canal in northeast Africa. The aim is to increase the amount of water in the Nile River by diverting water from the Sudd swamps in Sudan where much of it evaporates. Huge digging machines are being used to cut a deep channel for the water. Some experts believe that the project will provide much-needed irrigation water for farmland downstream. Others fear that the canal will turn the Sudd swamps into desert. A similar project in the southern Soviet Union has caused the Aral Sea, once the world's fourth-largest inland sea, to lose 69 percent of its water in less than 30 years. The shrinking of the Aral Sea has caused an ecological disaster affecting 30 million people.

Preserving the habitat

There are many organizations, at a local, national, and international level, devoted to preserving the environment. Together, they form the "Green movement." In several countries there are Green political parties.

Whenever a habitat is threatened by industry or development, the Green movement takes the side of the environment. These groups already enjoy considerable public support, but their most important work is education. Unless people understand how threats to the environment affect them, they cannot appreciate the importance of preserving habitats. Every hectare that we save today is one that will be enjoyed by our grandchildren.

▼ Natural grassland, with its springtime carpet of wild flowers, is becoming rare in Europe and North America. Unless action is taken to preserve the few remaining areas, the flowers will disappear under the plow.

Many farmers are sympathetic to the Green movement, despite the pressure to grow the maximum amount of food. Some make an effort to preserve small areas of woodland and hedgerow, and are careful not to spray these areas with pesticides. A few have turned their backs on modern methods and use no chemicals at all, either in fertilizers or pesticides.

Farming without chemicals is known as organic farming. In many countries, organic produce has become very popular. Because no chemicals are used to grow the food, there are none to enter the human food chain. In addition, by choosing organic produce, people think they are also choosing to save the countryside.

In the developing countries, action is finally being taken to save the rain forests. In Africa, the Ivory Coast recently banned all timber exports. In Central America, the government of Panama made it illegal to cut down any tree more than five years old. Such actions show great determination, because timber exports have been a major source of income.

It is difficult to persuade poor people in developing countries of the importance of saving the forests. They need more food and want to use the land to grow it on. But saving habitats is not a luxury, it is a necessity. What is at stake is not just our enjoyment of nature, but the future of life on Earth.

◀ Wicken Fen Nature Reserve in England. Wetlands, such as marshes and bogs, are extremely rich in rare plant and animal species. Unfortunately, they also make excellent farmland after they have been drained.

▼ Yellowstone National Park in the United States, famous for its grizzly bears and spectacular geysers. Most countries have established national parks where wildlife is protected and development is prohibited.

Species at risk

▶ The golden lion tamarin is a small monkey and is now very rare in the wild. It lives only in forest remnants in eastern Brazil. Hundreds have been exported for zoos and for the pet trade. This is now illegal, but still continues. The tamarins' habitat has been almost completely destroyed by development for the tourist trade.

When a species becomes extinct, it disappears for ever. Extinction is a natural part of evolution, but it is usually a slow process. Human beings speed things up. Some animals that are known from photographs taken during the last century are now extinct. Today, a huge international trade in animals and animal products is consuming the planet's wildlife. We are also destroying the habitats in which they live. Directly or indirectly, human activity now threatens many familiar species. Yet it is only through our intervention that many endangered species have any chance of survival at all. On the other hand, some wildlife species thrive in human company, but these are often the least welcome.

Animal products

Human beings have an insatiable appetite for animal protein. In China, where almost everything is considered edible, the wildlife is steadily being eaten to extinction. The world's oceans are under similar threat. Overfishing can cause dramatic changes in the size of marine populations. In 1937 California landed 750,000 metric tons of sardines; by 1957 this had fallen to a mere 17 metric tons. Such a rapid decrease in numbers creates a gap in natural food chains that can affect other species.

At the beginning of the last century, there were perhaps 40 million bison roaming the North American prairies. By 1900, only 500 remained. The vast majority of those slaughtered were left to rot. The hunters only wanted the hides for leather.

Many other species have been hunted to the point of extinction for their skins and furs. Countless beavers, otters, seals, minks, bears, and leopards and other big cats have been sacrificed in the name of fashion and status. Human fancies have created an international trade in animal products: exotic feathers for hats, turtle shells for combs, and recently the craze for rare and exotic pets.

Easy money is the motive. The poachers become rich, while the world becomes poorer. Several species of rhinoceros have disappeared because their horns were thought to have magic powers. Today, the African elephant is threatened because of its tusks. The ivory is considered valuable because it can be carved into souvenirs for tourists.

◀ These African zebra skins may be destined to upholster prestige furniture in Europe or North America. Most of the demand for furs and skins comes from the developed countries which have destroyed nearly all their own wildlife. Animal products are a valuable export commodity for many developing countries.

▼ These ivory carvings are made from the tusks of the African elephant. The population of African elephants has been dropping quickly, largely because of ivory poaching. Poaching gangs operate in game preserves despite armed patrols. These carvings were seized by customs, as exporting is illegal.

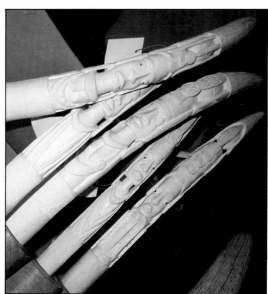

The march of extinction

Extinct and endangered wildlife

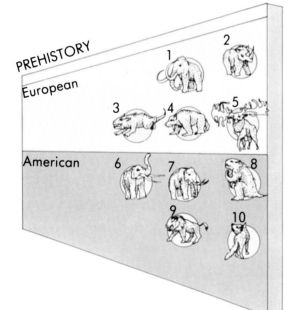

Recently discovered evidence suggests that early humans played an important role in the extinction of some prehistoric animals. During the last 500 years, people have certainly left their mark on the world's wildlife. Dozens of species known to our ancestors have now vanished. Only pictures and descriptions remain. Species that live on islands are more vulnerable than those on the mainland.

Perhaps the most frightening example is the passenger pigeon. During the early 1800s, a single flock was estimated to contain over 2 billion individuals. Through a combination of habitat destruction and hunting for food and sport, the bird had disappeared from the wild by the end of the century. The last passenger pigeon died in a zoo in 1914.

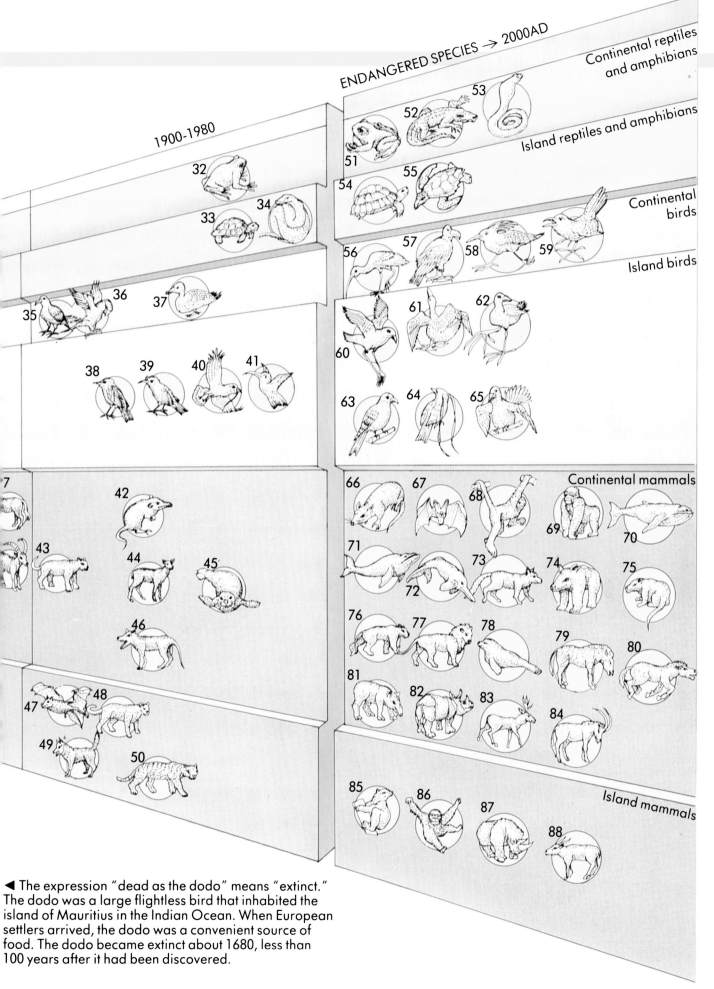

1900-1980

Continental reptiles and amphibians

Island reptiles and amphibians

Continental birds

Island birds

Continental mammals

Island mammals

◄ The expression "dead as the dodo" means "extinct." The dodo was a large flightless bird that inhabited the island of Mauritius in the Indian Ocean. When European settlers arrived, the dodo was a convenient source of food. The dodo became extinct about 1680, less than 100 years after it had been discovered.

31

On the edge

Today, some of the world's most familiar animal species stand at the edge of extinction. Over 6,000 species are officially acknowledged to be endangered, and the list is far from complete. Large animals are especially at risk from habitat destruction. Their natural populations tend to be quite small, because each individual requires proportionately more territory.

The African elephant is the world's largest land animal. During the last ten years, its numbers have been halved from 1.3 million to 600,000, by ivory poachers. Its smaller cousin, the Asiatic, or Indian, elephant, is reduced to about 30,000 individuals living in the wild.

Survival at sea

In the oceans, the aquatic mammals are perhaps most at risk. Twelve species of whale are endangered, and the gray whale has been saved from extinction only by 50 years of international protection. The one remaining species of dugong, or sea cow, is still being hunted in Indonesia. In the Mediterranean, the monk seal population is now less than 1,000.

Nor are human beings especially careful about their own close relatives. There are at least 50 species of primates in danger. The gorillas and the orangutans now exist only in very small numbers. Declining chimpanzee populations are causing concern throughout Africa. Many small animal species, such as the golden marmoset, are now seriously threatened by the growing demand for exotic pets.

Many extinctions have been caused by humans introducing animal predators. For the last 50 years, no offspring of one species of giant Galápagos tortoise have survived. The young are eaten by black rats which arrived on the Galápagos Islands with human settlers. Other unique island species are also threatened. In Madagascar, populations of some rare primates such as aye-ayes and lemurs number less than 100 individuals.

▶ The giant panda is found only in a small area of southern China. There are about 200 pandas left in the wild, and they very rarely breed in captivity. When the last wild panda dies, extinction will surely follow.

▲ The shy and gentle mountain gorilla is one of the world's rarest animals. Its habitat in West Africa is disappearing under the pressure of human cultivation. Tourists who are drawn to these remote areas to see wild gorillas are increasingly damaging the habitat.

◀ The southern right whale is one of the world's largest living animals. Formerly killed in large numbers, it is now "commercially extinct." This means that it is not worth the expense of hunting the last few. This has extended the species's life a little, but there may not be enough individuals left for the population to recover.

Saving species

◀ Przewalski's horse now exists only in captivity, but in sizable numbers. Zoologists would like to release some back into Central Asia, but they are concerned that the horse has become adapted to life in zoos.

▶ The white rhinoceros, like all rhinoceros species, is seriously endangered. In 1979 Project Rhino was launched to coordinate attempts to save them. Poachers are still a deadly threat to rhinoceroses.

▼ The Arabian oryx became extinct in the wild in 1972. Fortunately, Operation Oryx had already established a small herd in an American zoo, which bred successfully. During the late 1970s the oryx was released back into the wild.

Perhaps the most important thing we can do for endangered species is to recognize their plight. Publicity from concerned governments, and organizations such as the World Wildlife Fund (WWF), has done a great deal to raise public awareness. Intervening to solve the problem, however, is very difficult.

Zoos provide endangered species with a mixed blessing. Although care may be given to them in captivity, the methods of capture are not always so gentle. The normal way of "taking" a young mammal is to first kill its mother. With tropical birds, as many as 50 may be killed for every live specimen taken.

Game preserves, which protect animals and their natural habitat, are much more humane. But the habitat may be too inaccessible, and armed guards may be required. Many poachers will start a gun battle with the game wardens rather than be caught.

If the species will breed in zoos, there is hope that a population may eventually be released back into the wild. Some species, however, do not breed in captivity. In a few cases, entire wild populations have been carefully collected, and then transported to a less threatened habitat. Sometimes they have been released in a game preserve, but for others a remote island has offered the only chance of safety. But there are fewer and fewer wild places left where animals can be safe from our exploitation of the land.

In many parts of the world, governments and international organizations have successfully cooperated to protect endangered wildlife. A series of projects has given several species a fighting chance of survival. At the other end of the scale, important work is also done by small local groups devoted to saving a single plant or insect species. One of the most important lessons of ecology is that every species has its role to play in the balance of nature, and therefore every species is important.

Project Tiger

The Bali and Caspian tigers are now extinct. The Siberian and Javan tigers are unlikely to survive the century outside zoos. The Bengal tiger is the only species that is likely to survive in the wild. Project Tiger is the master plan for saving the Bengal tigers.

The Indian government, with support from the WWF, has established nine tiger reserves. Trained rangers and armed guards protect the animals against poachers and forest fires. Some animals are fitted with electronic collars to monitor their movements.

Thriving with people

Representatives of several animal groups — mammals, birds, and insects — have adapted to human existence so well that they have become pests. Most of them have completely abandoned a wild existence, and have become parasites on human food webs. From the time people began sailing the world, such animals have traveled around the globe in ships' cargoes. These species now live near people all over the world.

There are over 3,500 known species of cockroach. A few of these have become such close companions of people that "roaches" are now almost universally despised. Able to eat virtually anything, and resistant to insecticides, cockroaches spoil human food and spread disease. The oriental and German cockroaches have become a familiar sight in millions of homes around the world.

The house mouse originated in Central Asia, but has spread around the world. The species has found a niche in the nooks and crannies of human habitations. Maintaining a cautious and nocturnal existence, mice scavenge food from human supplies and waste. Their larger cousins, the brown and black rats, are far more destructive. Both rat and mice populations can undergo very rapid growth when conditions are good. These pests can consume huge quantities of stored food in homes and warehouses.

Larger woodland mammals are slowly coming to terms with humans, and the process is speeded up by the growth of suburbs. Raccoons or foxes are quite a common sight in country gardens, and both species are now adapting to life in the city. In parts of Alaska, polar bears are known to raid garbage cans.

Raccoon

Black-headed gull

Herring gull

House mouse

Brown rat

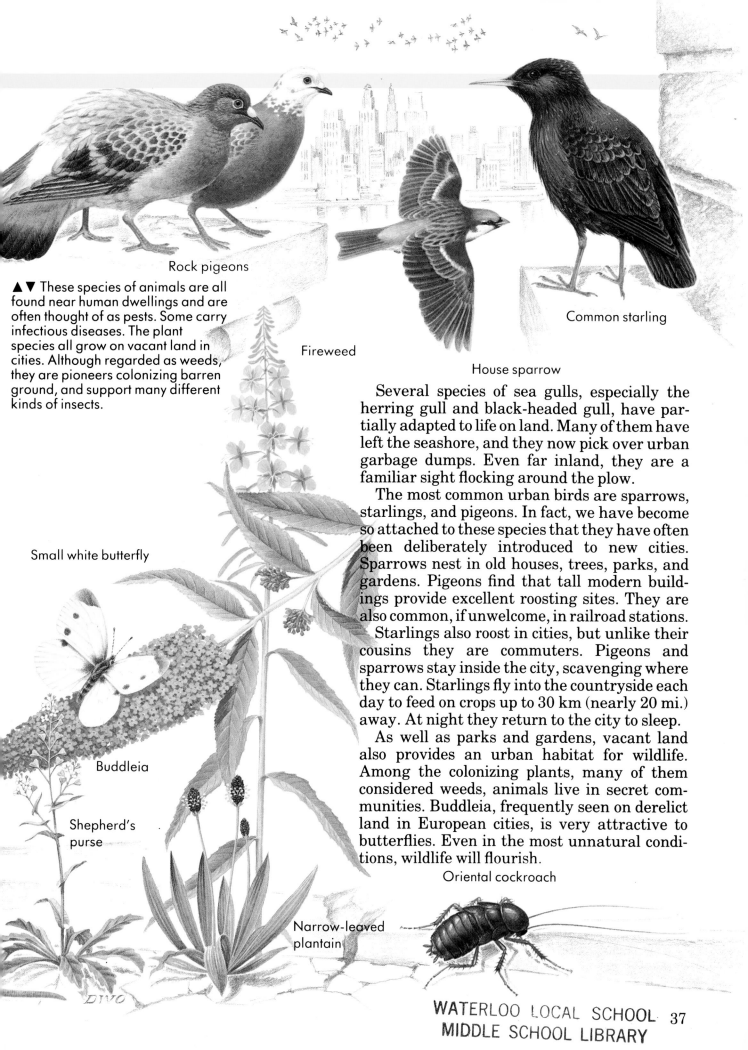

Rock pigeons

▲▼ These species of animals are all found near human dwellings and are often thought of as pests. Some carry infectious diseases. The plant species all grow on vacant land in cities. Although regarded as weeds, they are pioneers colonizing barren ground, and support many different kinds of insects.

Fireweed

Common starling

House sparrow

Small white butterfly

Buddleia

Shepherd's purse

Narrow-leaved plantain

Oriental cockroach

Several species of sea gulls, especially the herring gull and black-headed gull, have partially adapted to life on land. Many of them have left the seashore, and they now pick over urban garbage dumps. Even far inland, they are a familiar sight flocking around the plow.

The most common urban birds are sparrows, starlings, and pigeons. In fact, we have become so attached to these species that they have often been deliberately introduced to new cities. Sparrows nest in old houses, trees, parks, and gardens. Pigeons find that tall modern buildings provide excellent roosting sites. They are also common, if unwelcome, in railroad stations.

Starlings also roost in cities, but unlike their cousins they are commuters. Pigeons and sparrows stay inside the city, scavenging where they can. Starlings fly into the countryside each day to feed on crops up to 30 km (nearly 20 mi.) away. At night they return to the city to sleep.

As well as parks and gardens, vacant land also provides an urban habitat for wildlife. Among the colonizing plants, many of them considered weeds, animals live in secret communities. Buddleia, frequently seen on derelict land in European cities, is very attractive to butterflies. Even in the most unnatural conditions, wildlife will flourish.

Pollution

Spot facts

● *Each year 110 million metric tons of sulfur dioxide (a major cause of acid rain) are released into the atmosphere.*

● *Over 8,000 different pollutants have been identified in water taken from lakes.*

● *Cleaning up after the nuclear accident at Three Mile Island will cost over $1 billion.*

● *Pollution travels. Acidic chemicals can be carried 2,000 km (over 1,000 mi.) by the wind before falling to Earth as acid rain.*

● *800 years ago King Edward I of England imposed a death penalty on anyone found burning coal because it created noxious fumes.*

▶ *This western grebe is being cleaned of the sticky crude oil which prevents it from flying and feeding. Oil was spilled accidentally into San Francisco Bay, from a Standard Oil tanker. Emergency bird-cleaning teams can help rescue some seabirds after a large disaster such as this. Pollution of the sea, lakes, and rivers causes untold damage to wildlife.*

Human beings are a species that poisons its own habitat. If we think of our planet as a spaceship, then we are the crew and all the other species are passengers. In general, we behave irresponsibly, strewing the communal living quarters with garbage. Earth's atmosphere forms a protective cocoon around our spaceship, which uses it to store and recycle essential elements such as carbon and oxygen. Humans fill the air with pollution that turns the rain acidic, and threatens to alter the climate.

Pollution from fossil and nuclear fuels, from industry and agriculture, is slowly poisoning not only the air but also the land and water that we share with all living things.

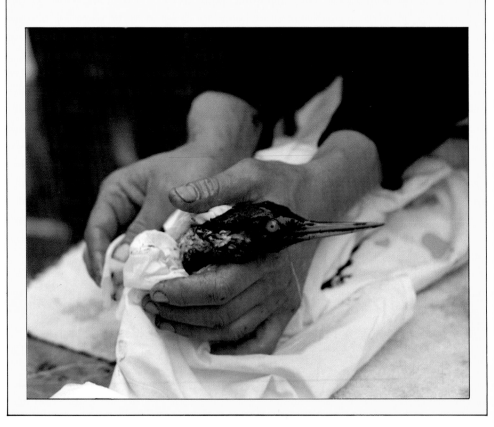

Poisoning the world

▲ Workers in protective clothing and masks clearing up after an explosion at a pesticide factory in Seveso, Italy. The ingredients of pesticides include some of the most poisonous chemicals we know.

◄ Mountains of solid waste disfigure the landscape. Little grows here. Metal and paper will eventually rust and rot, but some of the plastic will last for many years before it eventually decomposes.

All living organisms produce waste products. With all species except humans, these are safely recycled by the ecosphere. We alone produce unnatural waste, and we produce it in huge quantities. Atmospheric pollution began when human beings first discovered fire, but for thousands of years it had little impact on the environment. Serious problems started during the 1800s with the coal-burning factories of the Industrial Revolution. The smoke belching from their chimneys turned buildings and trees black with soot. Today, factory smoke is much "cleaner." The black soot has largely been eliminated, but invisible combustion products continue to pour into the air.

In the 20th century, huge numbers of motor vehicles have greatly increased the burden on the atmosphere. Vehicle exhaust fumes contain several harmful substances. These include carbon monoxide, a highly poisonous gas; nitrogen oxide, which produces acid rain; and lead, which is deadly to most forms of life. The volume of automobiles is steadily increasing.

Industry is responsible for a wide range of other pollutants. Many of the chemicals used in industry are poisonous, and others are known to cause cancer or deformities in babies. In many countries, especially in recent years, industry is very careful, but accidents do happen. A single chemical spillage can cause a river to become lifeless for years. Some companies have disposed of their waste chemicals by dumping them on empty land. This land is now completely uninhabitable.

Most modern farmers use large quantities of powerful chemicals to kill weeds and insects. Even in the dilute concentrations used in spraying, these can damage wildlife.

Some of these chemicals tend to accumulate in animals' bodies. The insecticide DDT is a notorious example. When such a chemical enters the food chain, it gets passed along. The higher up the food chain an animal is, the more chemicals it absorbs. This process is known as bioconcentration. Predators, such as birds of prey, are especially at risk.

Polluting the air

Each year millions of tons of pollution from power stations, factories, and automobiles enter the atmosphere. Most countries have agreed to reduce the pollution caused by industry. Some now require automobiles to be fitted with devices to filter out pollutants, or to use cleaner types of gasoline.

Despite these measures, the effects of atmospheric pollution are often felt below. Acid rain is created when the products of burning coal and oil, combustion products, become combined with water in the atmosphere to form acids. Falling back to Earth as rain, these acids directly attack trees and plants. Acidic water also accumulates in rivers and lakes, killing fish and other aquatic life. The acid destroys the natural chemical balance.

Over 60 percent of British forests have been harmed by acid rain, and large areas of North America are similarly affected. The winds often take acid rain to neighboring countries. Southern Norway, for example, has little heavy industry, yet 80 percent of its lakes are now devoid of life, or on the critical list.

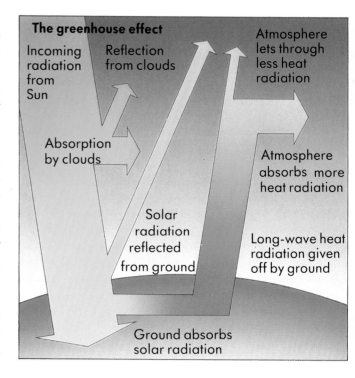

The greenhouse effect

Incoming radiation from Sun

Reflection from clouds

Atmosphere lets through less heat radiation

Absorption by clouds

Solar radiation reflected from ground

Atmosphere absorbs more heat radiation

Long-wave heat radiation given off by ground

Ground absorbs solar radiation

▲ Carbon dioxide has formed a blanket around the planet. Heat energy from the Sun is trapped by the atmosphere, which is slowly warming up.

Bhopal

Accidental air pollution by industrial chemicals can have disastrous local effects.

On December 3, 1984, there was an accident at a pesticide factory in the town of Bhopal, India. An explosion released 30 metric tons of methyl isocyanate, a highly toxic gas, into the air. Over 200,000 people in the vicinity were exposed to the gas. About 2,500 people were killed immediately, as many as 10,000 may have died subsequently, and at least 20,000 were disabled for life.

The Bhopal incident drew attention to one of the most important pollution issues. The rich countries of Europe and North America can afford to be concerned about pollution. They have well-developed industrial economies, and can impose high standards of safety and cleanliness. Poorer countries in the developing world often cannot afford to take these measures, even though they may wish to.

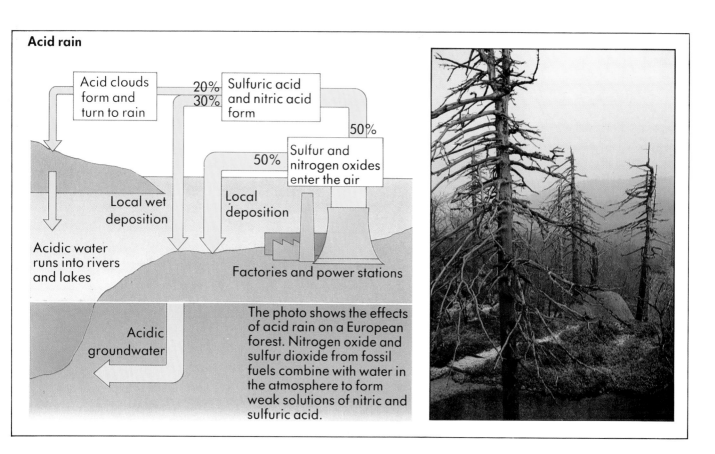

Acid rain

Acid clouds form and turn to rain

20%
30%
Sulfuric acid and nitric acid form

50%

50%
Sulfur and nitrogen oxides enter the air

Local wet deposition

Local deposition

Acidic water runs into rivers and lakes

Factories and power stations

Acidic groundwater

The photo shows the effects of acid rain on a European forest. Nitrogen oxide and sulfur dioxide from fossil fuels combine with water in the atmosphere to form weak solutions of nitric and sulfuric acid.

Human activity is producing far more carbon dioxide gas than the oceans and forests can recycle. On a global scale, increased amounts of carbon dioxide in the atmosphere threaten to change the climate of the whole planet. As the gas accumulates in the upper atmosphere it creates an insulating layer around the planet. Scientists believe that average temperatures on Earth might rise by 4°C (7°F). The ice caps could melt and many countries be flooded.

This problem is often called the greenhouse effect. Carbon dioxide from burning fuel is the main culprit, but other gases are also involved, notably chlorofluorocarbons (CFCs). CFCs are used in the United States in such things as coolants, cleaning solvents in the electronics industry, and insulating foams. CFCs are also dissolving the Earth's ozone layer. Without ozone to act as a filter, the Sun's rays can be harmful to living things.

◀ Smog over Mexico City. Fumes from the burning of fossil fuels can become trapped near the ground by a layer of air. The action of sunlight on the trapped fumes produces a poisonous smog.

41

Nuclear hazards

Radioactivity occurs naturally: many rocks are slightly radioactive. As life on Earth evolved, it adapted to this background radiation. Humans first discovered the secrets of nuclear power in the 1940s. Since then, pollution from unnatural radioactivity has become a potential health hazard. There has been considerable debate about what constitutes a safe dose of radiation. Today, most scientists agree that any exposure to unnatural radiation can be dangerous, and may usually be a risk not worth taking.

The world's first major exposure to radiation pollution followed the use and testing of atomic weapons. Nearly 1,500 bombs have been detonated, most of them in the atmosphere, although the earliest tests were made in deserts and on remote islands. These explosions have scattered tons of radioactive fallout around the world. Some of the fallout loses its radiation within a short time. But some of the radioactive substances, or radioisotopes, remain dangerous for many years.

These isotopes enter food chains via plants, and can accumulate in animal bodies and be passed along food chains. In the past there was considerable concern about the amount of the isotope strontium-90 in cows' milk. International agreement has now almost put an end to atomic tests.

Today, the use of nuclear power to generate electricity is the main focus of concern. Although nuclear power stations are designed to be as safe as possible, there is always some leakage of radiation during operation. There is also the problem of what to do with the radioactive fuel after use. Additionally, there is always the possibility of an accident.

▼ A reactor at the Three Mile Island power station in Pennsylvania has been shut down since an accident there on March 28, 1979. Mechanical failure caused the reactor to overheat, which might have led to a far greater catastrophe. After 18 hours, engineers were able to bring the reactor under control and so avert the danger of a deadly explosion.

There have been two major accidents at nuclear power stations. In 1979, a pump failed at the Three Mile Island installation in the United States. The operators managed to prevent an explosion, but the reactor was wrecked and a considerable amount of radiation was released into the atmosphere.

In 1986, their Soviet counterparts were not so successful, and a reactor at the Chernobyl power station exploded. The explosion produced a cloud of fallout that spread over 75 percent of Europe. Even in Sweden, thousands of kilometers from Chernobyl, livestock had to be kept under cover to protect it from the fallout. Experts predict that at least 1,000 people in Western Europe will die as a result of eating food contaminated by the fallout.

These two accidents have caused many people, and some governments, to have second thoughts about nuclear power. There will always be a risk, and the next accident might be much worse.

▲ Checking vegetables with a Geiger counter, which measures radioactivity. Meat and milk products gave the most concern after Chernobyl. In Great Britain, a ban was put on the sale of sheep from areas that received the heaviest fallout: over 500 farms were still affected a year later.

◄ When the nuclear reactor at Chernobyl exploded in 1986, it blew apart the entire building and started a fire. Some of the first casualties were firemen who received fatal doses of radiation while bravely fighting the blaze. At least 300 Soviets may have so far died as a result of the explosion, and many towns and villages have been permanently evacuated.

Polluting the water

All the waters of the Earth are bombarded with pollutants. Rain and rivers wash our waste into lakes and seas, where it slowly accumulates. Natural processes can remove some, but by no means all, of the pollutants that household and industrial waste contains.

In Europe, the Rhine River alone carries over 300,000 metric tons of waste into the North Sea each year. Most of this is permitted waste: sewage and waste chemicals that most scientists believe the sea can safely absorb. But a series of accidents have also spilled many tons of highly poisonous substances.

Cities and industry are not the only cause of water pollution. The artificial fertilizers that many farmers depend on can also pollute water supplies. The phosphates and nitrates contained in artificial fertilizer are easily washed out of the soil by rain. These nutrient chemicals accumulate in rivers and lakes, where they destroy the natural balance of nutrients.

▲ The first oil tanker disaster to affect Great Britain was the wreck of the *Torrey Canyon* in 1967. After other measures failed, the government had the wreck bombed, to prevent further pollution.

▲ (inset) In 1978 an oil spill from the tanker *Amoco Cadiz* devastated part of the French coastline. A national emergency was declared, and clean-up operations lasted for months.

◄ Several countries continue to pump chemical wastes and untreated sewage into the sea. Many beaches have been declared unfit for swimming because of the potential health risks from this pollution.

The increased concentrations of nutrients stimulate algae (microscopic water plants) to overgrow. When the nutrient resources are all used up, the algae die. As they decompose, all the oxygen in the water is used up and the environment becomes lifeless.

This process, which is known as eutrophication, usually occurs in small bodies of water. Recently, however, it has been blamed for the great masses of dead algae that have been observed in some of the world's smaller seas.

Enclosed seas, such as the Mediterranean Sea and the Baltic Sea, are particularly at risk from water pollution. Their coasts are lined with industry, and they have only narrow outlets into the main oceans. Pollution therefore becomes more concentrated, and the effects on marine life are much greater. These seas may soon become completely dead.

Oil is probably Earth's most valuable and useful commodity, and hundreds of millions of tons are carried by tankers each year. Inevitably there have been accidents, and large quantities of crude oil have spilled into the sea.

Crude oil floats on the surface, and decomposes in a few weeks under the action of seawater and sunlight. When the spill occurs close to land, and oil is washed ashore, a few weeks is far too long. The oil coats everything and has a disastrous effect on the local ecosystem. Seabirds and aquatic mammals sink and drown, shellfish are smothered, and many fish are poisoned.

Water pollution has spread to the poles, and has now entered the Antarctic food chains. Many scientists think that the choice is quite simple: either we clean up, and halt the increase in pollution, or our planet will slowly die.

Part Two

Agriculture

The human population of planet Earth has doubled during the last 40 years. Increased demand for food has led to a "Green Revolution" in world agriculture. Despite employing the most modern and intensive techniques, parts of the world have vast surpluses of food, while other parts have too little.

Our crops and livestock, and the methods used to raise them, have remained little changed throughout most of history. Over the last 50 years, the application of science has brought the farmer new varieties of plants and animals that can produce food more efficiently. Science has also created the artificial substances that support and protect these new crops and animals. Fears about continuing pollution, and widespread criticism of some farming methods, have placed agriculture in the spotlight of world opinion. Many people now believe that we must change our approach to feeding the world.

◄ A field of wheat ripens in the sun. Wheat and other cereal crops provide most of our food. New strains of wheat have kept pace with the demands of our growing population.

Feeding the world

Spot facts

● About 85 percent of the world's food comes from just 20 different plant species.

● Agriculture accounts for more than 70 percent of the world's annual water consumption in the form of irrigation.

● On average between sixty and eighty thousand people starve to death each day.

● The United States uses over 125 kg of artificial fertilizer per hectare (110 lb. per acre) of cultivated land every year.

● Great Britain has more farm tractors (300,000) than farm workers (250,000).

● Women grow over half of the world's food. In Africa, they grow 75 percent of it.

▶ Mothers and children in Ethiopia eating the daily rations provided by famine relief agencies. Today, the world produces enough food to feed an additional billion people, but people still die from hunger. The problems of world hunger are largely the result of inefficient distribution.

Nearly all of the world's food comes from agriculture, the deliberate cultivation of plant and animal species. Agriculture exploits the natural processes of growth and reproduction, but people have increasingly altered the course of nature in order to feed our unnaturally large population.

In general, the development of agricultural techniques has been a gradual process. Much of the world's food is still grown using methods that have not altered in centuries. But during the last 40 years global food production has doubled. Most of the increase has been due to the application of modern scientific techniques, such as selective breeding and the introduction of machinery, artificial fertilizers, and pesticides.

Early days

Civilization requires a settled existence. Towns and cities depend upon a surplus from the fields to feed populations that are not growing their own food. The development of civilized skills, such as reading, writing, and painting, in turn depends upon urban populations freed from daily labor in the fields.

The most primitive form of human life-style is that of the hunter-gatherers. Wild animals are trapped and hunted for meat and skins, but fruits, nuts, and seeds gathered from the wild provide the basis of daily existence. Hunter-gatherers are always in danger of outgrowing their food supply. If there are too many mouths to feed, the available food resources can quickly be used up.

Agriculture developed from attempts to improve this precarious life-style, and probably began with the domestication of the first food animals. Wild sheep and goats were collected into herds and managed, rather than being hunted and killed.

▲ A 3,000-year-old Egyptian wall painting. The artist has depicted typical farming activities, such as plowing and harvesting, together with a wide range of crops, including grains, fruit, and vegetables.

Animal herders have a nomadic existence; they must be constantly on the move in search of fresh pasture. Long-term human settlement, such as the first permanent cities, became possible only when we discovered how to domesticate and cultivate nutritious plants.

The earliest evidence of cultivation comes from the Middle East around 8,000 years ago. About that time, the ancestors of wheat and barley were first sown in fields that were worked entirely by hand. In Mexico, maize (corn) was grown about 6,500 years ago, and in China rice was first cultivated around 5,000 years ago.

In ancient Egypt, irrigation water provided by the annual flooding of the Nile River enabled farmers to produce large surpluses of food.

49

Ancient and modern

The two most primitive forms of agriculture still in existence are nomadic herding and tropical slash-and-burn cultivation. Neither requires any specialized technology, but neither is capable of producing a large food surplus. Increased productivity became possible only through the introduction of new technology such as the plow.

The ox-drawn plow was in use before 2500 BC, and the ox remained the main work animal until about 1000 AD, when the horse collar was invented. Horsepower became dominant in Western agriculture, although in other regions oxen and cattle are still used. In many parts of Asia, Africa, and South America, the hoe remains the main agricultural implement. In the developed world, the introduction of machinery and the invention of the tractor and combine harvester greatly improved agricultural output.

The ability to produce a surplus frees farmers from "subsistence agriculture," growing just enough to feed the family. Instead, they may grow a little extra to sell. This is a "cash crop." Today, about half the world's food, and many other substances, are produced as cash crops by specialist farmers. The remainder of our food is produced by millions of subsistence farmers.

▲ Sudanese tribesmen threshing sorghum, a coarse grain. Primitive agriculture requires no tools other than a digging stick, which doubles as a threshing club. Often the crops receive little or no attention between planting and harvest. Sorghum and millet are the main cereal crops in dry tropical countries.

◄ Planting crops in Brazil, on land cleared by the slash-and-burn method, an effective technique for forcing a good crop from poor forest soils. Burning the trees releases nutrients, in the form of wood ash, back into the soil. Growing crops make good use of these but the soil is left exhausted. After one harvest, the land must be left at least 30 years for the forest to regrow in order to recover its fertility. Slash-and-burn agriculture is also practiced in tropical Africa and Southeast Asia.

Efficiency in agriculture is a very difficult concept to define. At the most basic level, it is the amount of food (the yield) that can be obtained from a certain area of land. In this sense, the new hybrid crops are much more efficient than any of the traditional varieties. A more precise definition of efficiency also needs to take into account the costs of producing the crop in terms of irrigation, fertilizer, and labor.

The type of crop is also important. Soybeans, for example, are about 10 times more efficient at producing protein than cattle. But Western tastes still demand meat, and much of the soybean crop goes to feed the cattle. They are a more desirable food product, despite the expensive use of land. Western farming is considered the most efficient type of agriculture, but there are some serious disadvantages. For example, pollution from agricultural chemicals has now entered water supplies, which may be dangerous.

▲ Aerial spraying is often used to spread artificial fertilizer and pesticide over large fields. The technique wastes a great deal of chemicals, but is considered efficient because it saves time and labor costs.

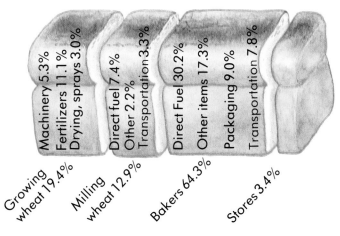

Growing wheat 19.4%
Machinery 5.3%
Fertilizers 11.1%
Drying, sprays 3.0%

Milling wheat 12.9%
Direct fuel 7.4%
Other 2.2%
Transportation 3.3%

Bakers 64.3%
Direct Fuel 30.2%
Other items 17.3%
Packaging 9.0%
Transportation 7.8%

Stores 3.4%

▲ Just under 20 percent of the total energy required to produce a loaf of white bread is consumed in growing the wheat. Over 60 percent is accounted for by the baking, packaging, and shipping.

Selective breeding

Selective breeding is as old as domestication itself. Humans have influenced the evolution of other species by tending only those plants and animals with desirable characteristics. Weak and diseased individuals have been removed from domesticated populations.

By 1930, the breeds and varieties used in agriculture were the result of centuries of luck, folk wisdom, and fashion. During the last 50 years, the application of genetic science has given us the power to shape plants and animals more precisely to fit our needs.

A worldwide breeding program, involving researchers as far apart as Chile and Japan, has produced a series of improved cereal varieties. Some have provided an immediate 20 percent increase in yield; others ripen during shorter summers, or resist certain plant diseases. These hybrid varieties now dominate world production. In the case of wheat, average yield has increased threefold. Other crops have received similar attention, and scientists are currently trying to introduce insect-repellent genes from a wild potato into ordinary cultivated varieties.

The demands of the meat-eating populations in Europe and America slowly changed during the last century. Animal fat was no longer needed to make candles, and increased vegetable oil production meant that less fat was needed as food. What people wanted was lean meat.

Animal breeding programs have pioneered many modern techniques. The first test-tube babies were, in fact, calves. The widespread use of artificial insemination has allowed a rapid transformation of livestock populations. Modern beef cattle have a higher ratio of muscle to bone, and our dairy herds produce more milk. Our pigs are leaner, and our sheep produce more lambs and wool. But they lead unnatural lives, supported by the increasing use of drugs.

These new techniques have played a major role in boosting animal productivity to its present limits. Further changes will be possible with the application of genetic engineering to food animals.

The Green Revolution

The new hybrid crops produced bumper harvests in Europe and the United States during the 1950s. During the 1960s they were introduced into many developing countries. By 1979 more than 50 million hectares (120 million acres) had been planted with hybrid seeds. The result was a Green Revolution that greatly increased productivity without extra land being cultivated.

In India, cereal production doubled in less than 20 years; in th e Philippines the rice yield went up by 75 percent. As well as producing more grain per hectare, the high-yield varieties mature more quickly. Some rice farmers are now able to achieve three crops per year.

Between 1950 and 1990, the Earth's human population doubled, and so did agricultural output. The Green Revolution has enabled the Earth to continue to feed the human population, but at a price.

Many of the new varieties will perform well only if they receive the artificial fertilizers that are commonplace in developed countries. These must be paid for, often as expensive imports, along with pesticides and other additives. The widespread use of agrochemicals in developing countries is now a significant factor in global pollution.

Triticale (right), a hybrid of wheat and rye, was developed during the 1950s, and was the first completely new crop for thousands of years. It is now a high-yield grain crop in many countries.

▲ Hybrid maize (corn) growing in a genetic engineering laboratory in California. Genetic engineering allows scientists to alter a plant species without crossbreeding thousands of individual plants.

Santa Gertrudis

Kankrej

▲ The Santa Gertrudis breed was developed by crossbreeding shorthorns with Brahmans, or zebus, like the Kankrej. Both do well in hot climates, but the Santa Gertrudis is farmed for beef in Texas, while the Kankrej is a draft animal in India.

53

Crop farming

The crops in our fields are the plant species that we have selected for cultivation. Many crops are restricted by climate to those parts of the world where they originated. Others have been transported around the world by human colonists.

The most important crops are known as staples and form the bulk of daily food intake. The staple crop varies in different parts of the world, but in most places it is one of the crops known as cereals.

Fruits and vegetables are usually grown to add variety to our diet, although some, such as potatoes and legumes, are also highly nutritious foods. Other crops are grown to provide basic ingredients, luxury items, like tea and coffee, or raw materials such as fibers.

► Terraced rice paddies in the Philippines. Terracing is a useful way of conserving valuable water, and making more land available for farming. Crops such as vines and olive trees are also grown on terraced hillsides in other parts of the world. Water can also be conserved on flat land by building low stone walls around crops.

The farming year

In all parts of the world, the rhythm of farming is dictated by the growing cycle of the main crop. Most of our crops are annual plants. Harvesting food often means taking the seeds, and these crops have to be sown afresh each year. Some, notably rice, have a very short growth period, and in the right climate can be sown more than once a year. Others, like fruit trees, supply an annual harvest for years.

Farming removes much greater amounts of water and nutrients from the soil than natural vegetation. In many countries, the supplying of additional water, through irrigation, is an essential feature of agriculture. Rice cultivation depends on irrigation by flooding, but for other crops, such as corn, spraying is the most common method, although it is extremely wasteful of water.

Traditionally, nutrients have been replaced by applying natural fertilizers, or by letting the land rest and lie fallow for a year. The most common natural fertilizers are manure and compost from decaying vegetation. Letting land lie fallow slowly developed into systems of crop rotation. Some crops, such as clover, are useful only for animal grazing, but are very efficient at putting nutrients back into the soil.

The widespread use of artificial fertilizers in the 20th century has transformed agriculture. Farmers can now grow the same crop on the same land year after year, without exhausting it. Chemical weed killers have also made the farmer's task much easier, as has the increased use of machines. But crop farming is still hard work. The land must be prepared each year, and crops must be tended at all stages of growth.

▼ Crop farming in the Western world is based on the growing cycle of the staple crop, in this case wheat. In the warmer regions, winter wheat can be sown in the fall. Where the winter frosts are cold enough to kill the developing plants, spring wheat is sown, to be harvested in late summer. Seeds are sown by a machine called a seed drill, and crops are harvested by a combine. Crops are top-dressed with fertilizer and pesticide.

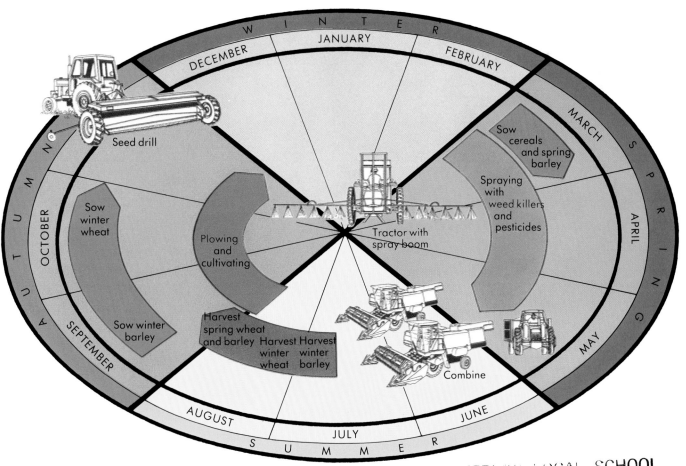

Cereals

Cereals, the grain-producing plants, are our most important crops. The world produces over 1.5 billion metric tons of cereal grains each year. Cereals are an ideal human foodstuff, mostly carbohydrates but containing 6 to 11 percent protein. Without these essential crops we could not even begin to feed the world.

Wheat is the most common cereal. In the form of bread or pasta, cooked wheat is the staple food of more than a third of the world's population. Most of our wheat is grown in the temperate climates of Eurasia and America, but it is also widely cultivated in India, China, and Australasia.

Wheat is most productive when farmed extensively in large open fields covering hundreds of hectares. Under these conditions, modern machinery, such as combines, can operate at maximum efficiency.

Wheat farming in the developed countries is now almost completely mechanized. In Africa and Asia, wheat is generally grown in much smaller fields that are sown and harvested by hand. Small farmers often lack machinery.

Rice is the staple cereal of tropical Asia, and requires a unique system of wet cultivation. Modern rice is not a seasonal crop, but the plant must be submerged in water for about 75 percent of its growing period. Rice cultivation creates a distinctive landscape of flooded paddy fields. Mechanization is difficult, especially on terraces, because of potential damage to paddy walls and the submerged crop. The water buffalo is far more important than the tractor, and human labor is most important of all.

Maize (corn) originated in South America, where it is still grown by traditional methods. It is also grown as food in parts of Africa. In the developed countries it is cultivated using modern machinery, and is mainly used for animal feed.

Millet is the world's fourth most important cereal, and is a staple crop in the drier regions of Asia and Africa. Rye, oats, and barley are grown in areas such as northern Europe, which have a cool damp climate. These three grains are little used as human foodstuffs, and nearly all the harvest goes for animal feed.

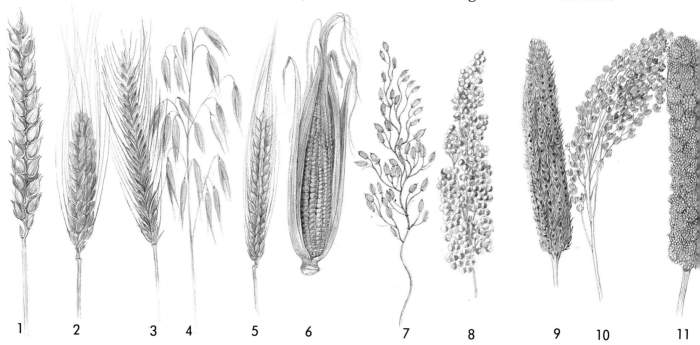

1   2   3   4   5   6   7   8   9   10   11

▲ The true cereals are all members of the grass family and are grown all over the world. Corn (maize) is most important in America, wheat in Europe, and rice in the tropics. The other cereals are of great importance in many countries in Africa.

Key
1 Bread wheat
2 Hard (durum) wheat
3 Rye
4 Oats
5 Six-row barley
6 Maize
7 Rice
8 Sorghum
9 Finger millet
10 Common millet
11 Foxtail millet

▲ A rice harvest in Nepal. Some of the new varieties of rice are faster growing as well as giving a higher yield. Some farmers can now grow three harvests per year. Such results depend on "supporting" the crop with artificial fertilizers and pesticides, and many farmers cannot afford these expensive chemicals. Although more food is now grown on the same amount of land, on average it costs more to produce.

▲ Rice is one of the very few crops that requires constant irrigation. The cultivation of rice is mainly limited to river valleys with a year-round supply of water. Individual farms usually cover less than 20 hectares (50 acres) because of the amount of work involved. Each rice seedling must be planted by hand, and so fields remain limited to the size a family can work in a day. Fish and ducks are traditionally raised in paddies alongside the rice plants.

◄ Wheat is grown on every continent. Asia is the world's leading producer, but the North American prairies produce the greatest surplus. Wheat farming in northwestern Europe is the most productive with yields up to 15 metric tons per hectare (2½ acres).

The huge machines used for intensive wheat production create a landscape with few obstructions. On hills, contour farming may help prevent soil erosion by rainwater.

Fruit

Fruits and vegetables provide variety, vitamins, and roughage to diets that would otherwise consist of carbohydrates and protein. A few are grown as subsistence crops, and potatoes and cassava have become staples in some countries. Others, such as pineapples and bananas, are grown as cash crops or, like turnips, as winter feed for livestock.

Different crops are cultivated for different parts of the plant. In general, the seeds and fruits are the most nutritious parts, but the leaves, stems, and roots of some are also eaten.

Fruits are usually cultivated as a plantation crop. An orchard is just a less intensive form of plantation agriculture, and is more suited to temperate climates. Harvesting fruit is extremely labor-intensive, as great care must be taken not to damage the crop. For this reason, fruit is usually an expensive luxury item. Tropical fruit is often picked before it is ripe so that it will remain fresh during transportation. It is shipped in refrigerated containers. Worldwide, an increasing amount of fruit is now grown for processing, especially into juice.

Some common tropical fruits

1 Pineapple 2 Durian 3 Carambola 4 Mango
5 Papaya 6 Soursop 7 Persimmon 8 Mangosteen 9 Pomegranate 10 Litchi 11 Akee 12 Cherimoya
13 Banana 14 Guava 15 Sapodilla 16 Passion fruit
17 Loquat 18 Cape gooseberry 19 Rambutan

Some common temperate fruits

1 Black currant 2 Red currant 3 Bilberry 4 Blueberry
5 Sweet cherry 6 Cranberry 7 Black mulberry
8 Gooseberry 9 Raspberry 10 Plum 11 Strawberry
12 Fig 13 Damson 14 Greengage 15 Medlar
16 Quince 17 Apricot 18 Peach 19 Apple 20 Pear

Vegetables

Vegetables generally require less preparation and care than other crops, and are the main component of kitchen gardens all over the world. Some fruits and salad vegetables are now grown commercially in greenhouses. Spain is particularly successful at this. By exercising control over the growing conditions, farmers can cultivate these crops out of season. Other vegetables are also raised as cash crops. In Europe and the United States, for example, fresh green peas have become a rarity. Nearly all go for canning and freezing.

The most useful vegetables are the legumes. This is a group of plants that includes peas, beans, lentils, and soybeans. As well as providing much more protein than cereals, legumes also put nutrients back into the soil. One of the ways agriculture could be improved is to make greater use of these plants.

Other future advances will probably involve making use of new crops. These include the winged bean, of which all parts can be eaten, and the yeheb bush, which produces nutritious seeds in arid conditions.

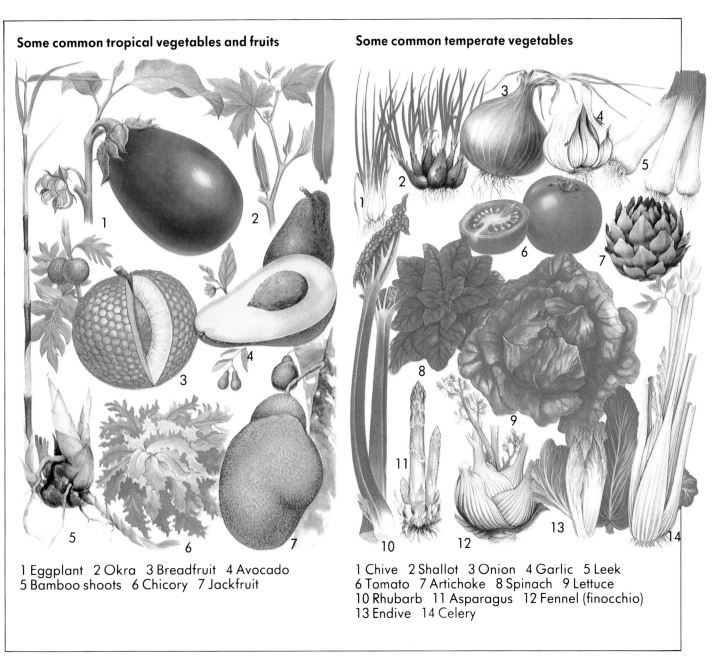

Some common tropical vegetables and fruits

1 Eggplant 2 Okra 3 Breadfruit 4 Avocado
5 Bamboo shoots 6 Chicory 7 Jackfruit

Some common temperate vegetables

1 Chive 2 Shallot 3 Onion 4 Garlic 5 Leek
6 Tomato 7 Artichoke 8 Spinach 9 Lettuce
10 Rhubarb 11 Asparagus 12 Fennel (finocchio)
13 Endive 14 Celery

Sugar and oil

Sugar

Table sugar became commonplace only about 300 years ago, when sugarcane was introduced into America. Before this time, honey was the major source of sugar, and bees were widely kept. Sugarcane is native to Southeast Asia, but it is now grown in most tropical and subtropical countries. Growth is limited only by the availability of water.

Sugarcane grows in tightly packed stands that reach an average of 6 m (20 ft.) in height. After harvesting, which is generally done by hand, the sugary sap is squeezed out in a roller mill. The sap is then boiled to make molasses. Further processing is required to produce the familiar white sugar crystals.

About 66 percent of world sugar production now comes from cane, but in Europe, the Soviet Union, and the United States, the sugar beet is also very important. The sugar beet is the result of a breeding program of the 1700s to improve natural beets, and the plant now has a 20 percent sugar content.

In some tropical countries, brown sugars are manufactured from dates and other palms, but these are mainly for local consumption.

Oil

From the earliest times, certain plants have provided oil for cooking and lighting. Until the 1800s, vegetable oils were almost the only type available to industry. Today, a very wide range of crops are grown for their oil. In all cases, the oil is squeezed out of the seeds or fruit, and the residue used as animal feed.

The commercial farming of oil-producing plants received a tremendous boost from the invention of margarine toward the end of the 1800s. During the last 20 years, vegetable oils have received a further boost, as increased health consciousness has led many people to consume less animal fat.

In tropical regions of Africa and Asia, especially in Indonesia and Malaysia. the oil palm is widely cultivated for cooking oil. The oil extracted from dried coconuts is also a valuable commodity, but it is mainly used industrially.

In Mediterranean climates, the olive is the main oil producer. Like the date palm, olive trees require little attention for most of the year, but harvesting is very hard work. Olive oil is not widely used outside the producing areas, because there are cheaper alternatives.

▲ In Spain, and other Mediterranean countries, olive trees are grown on hillside terraces for their valuable oil. Olive trees are very slow-growing.

◄ Sugarcane being harvested (far left) and processed (left) at a sugar factory in Barbados. After crushing, the cane can be processed into paper, and the molasses residue makes excellent animal feed.

► Rape is grown as a forage or cover crop and also for the oil in its seeds. Its oil is edible but has a very unpleasant smell. The crushed seeds go to make cattle feed.

Fiber and beverage crops

Fiber crops

A few crops are grown primarily for the useful fibers that can be extracted from various parts of the plant. Plant fibers have been used for centuries to make cloth, canvas, carpets, and rope. For many applications, however, they have now been replaced by artificial fibers, such as rayon and nylon.

Fibers from seeds, stems, fruits, and leaves are all used. Some fiber crops also provide oil and animal feed. The most important fiber crops are grown in tropical and subtropical regions, often on large plantations.

Cotton is the world's leading fiber crop, and is grown in more than 60 countries. The major producers are the United States, the Soviet Union, China, Korea, India, Brazil, and Egypt. The fibers are taken from the top of the plant, where they surround and protect the seeds in the cotton boll, or seedpod.

Since 1800, the process of extracting the seeds from the fibers, known as ginning, has been mechanized. In other respects, cotton is still a very demanding crop, requiring constant attention. In the United States, Mexico, and the Soviet Union, the cultivation of large fields is aided by machines. Elsewhere, cotton cultivation requires a large labor force.

Until very recently, jute was second only to cotton in importance. Jute is a tall plant, 2-5 m (7-16 ft.) high, with strong fibers in the stem. Today, jute fiber has mainly been replaced by plastic, but it is still important for twine, and in the upholstery and carpet industries.

Flax is grown both to produce the fine tough fiber of linen cloth, and for linseed oil. The plant grows well in cool, moist climates, and Europe and the Soviet Union are the major producers.

Several plants from the agave family are grown for the tough fibers in their leaves. The most important yield the fibers known as sisal, which is mainly grown in Central America, but is also cultivated in East Africa and Indonesia.

Other fiber crops include hemp, which was once grown for rope; kapok, collected from the seeds of a tropical tree; and ramie, a grass grown in China and used both for clothing and for making paper.

Coffee and tea

Coffee and tea have no food value, yet they are two of the world's most valuable agricultural commodities. Several countries depend on one or other of these crops to maintain their national economies.

Our 300-year-old appetite for morning coffee is now met largely from South America, and Brazil alone supplies about half the world's consumption. Coffee is also widely cultivated in East Africa. After harvest, the bright red coffee berries must be dried and skinned in order to reveal the coffee "beans." Most of the beans are now processed and sold as instant coffee.

Tea originated in Southeast Asia, where it has been drunk for thousands of years. It was introduced into Europe in the 1700s. Today, India, Sri Lanka, and China produce about 60 percent of world production. Large quantities are also exported from Indonesia and East Africa. Growing on the bush, tea leaves are 5-8 cm (2-3 in.) long. These are crushed and dried before being packed for shipping.

► A worker in Uganda picking the ripe red berries from a coffee bush. Each berry contains two seeds, or beans. Machines remove the pulpy flesh surrounding the beans, which are then dried. Next the hulls, or coverings, of the beans are removed, producing what is called green coffee. Roasting the green coffee beans allows them to develop their rich flavor.

▲ In Peru, South America, a cotton picker sorts through a mass of freshly picked cotton, removing twigs and leaves. The fluffy "snowballs" of cotton still contain the seeds, which are later removed during ginning. Yarn is spun from long cotton fibers, called lint. Short fibers, called linters, are used to make absorbent cotton, and are a raw material for making rayon.

▶ Picking tea on a large plantation in Tanzania, East Africa. The tea plant is a small shrub, which is kept well pruned so that it keeps producing fresh young leaves. For black tea, the leaves are allowed to wilt for a day or two before being crushed. Then they ferment in the air, which makes them turn black. The fermentation process is stopped by heating them in an oven.

Cattle farming

▶ Zebu cattle on a ranch in Brazil. Originating from India, zebus are well suited to subtropical climates. The distinctive hump is thought to have been selected for by centuries of use as draft animals. Yoking the cattle is made easier by the hump. In India, the cow is considered a sacred animal and is not exploited for meat.

Cattle are the world's most important agricultural animals, providing high-quality meat, milk, and muscle power. Beefsteak is widely considered to be a luxury food, and in some less developed countries, cows are still an important symbol of wealth and status. Cattle have least agricultural importance in the rice-growing areas, and in India they are used only for milk and as draft animals. Both beef and dairy farming became global industries when canning and refrigeration were invented during the 1800s. By 1900, beef and butter were being traded around the world. One of the major uses of beef in Western countries is for hamburger.

Raising cattle

There are three basic kinds of cattle: longhorn, shorthorn, and humped zebu. All share a common ancestor, the aurochs, now extinct.

Today, commercial cattle farming is either intensive, as in northern Europe, or extensive, as on the cattle ranches of the American West. In East and West Africa, sizable numbers of cattle are kept by nomadic herders.

Cattle ranching requires large areas of land with year-round natural grazing, and was once confined to temperate grasslands. Ranching is now established in South and Central America on land cleared from rain forest.

Methods of cattle rearing

A rancher needs to be extremely mobile, hence the partnership between people and horses. The "cowboy" has existed in various parts of the world for over a thousand years, first in North Africa, then later in Spain, America, and Australasia. However, the modern cowboy is as likely to ride a motorcycle as a horse.

Where land is at a premium, cattle are raised intensively. In countries such as Great Britain, Holland, Denmark, and Germany, cattle are kept indoors during the winter and fed on stored fodder such as hay. Modern intensive production requires that the animals be kept indoors for most, if not all, of the year. They may be fed a combination of grain, root crops, cabbages, and "cakes" or meal made from oil seeds. In the United States many cattle are raised intensively, especially near big cities.

The ratio of cattle to land varies greatly. In Australia, where the grazing is quite poor, the average density is only four animals per square kilometer (about 250 acres, or 2/5 sq. mi.). In the United States, where both intensive and extensive methods are used, the average density is the same as that for the whole world, at 25 animals per sq km. In Holland, cattle are raised at an average density of 180 animals per sq km.

▶ Young beef cattle being fattened up for sale on a farm in California. When cattle are raised intensively for meat, the animals themselves require very little room or human labor. However, in terms of the land required to grow their feed, the cattle indirectly occupy a much larger area. There is also the problem of disposing of the animals' waste.

Dairy cattle

Cattle provide us with more than eight times as much food in the form of milk as in the form of meat. Nearly all commercial milk production comes from intensive farming. Because cows require milking twice daily, dairy cattle cannot be spread over large areas. Only in New Zealand is the grazing of sufficient quality to allow extensive dairy farming.

Cattle are raised for milk in most parts of the world, often on the basis of one cow per village. The main areas of commercial dairy production are in Europe and North America. The traditional dairy herd was quite small because milking by hand is a very slow and tiring process. Ten cows were all that a single person could handle.

The development of the milking machine allowed a single farm worker to milk up to 80 cattle. The modern milking parlor, together with the introduction of year-round shelter and improved animal feed, has transformed dairy farming. Nowadays it is an extremely productive industry.

Most breeds of cattle can be raised for both beef and milk, but shorthorn dairy breeds give much higher milk yields.

▼ The best dairy breeds provide excellent milk but are much too skinny for commercial meat production. The Brown Swiss has been used to improve dairy herds in the United States. The Jersey is a small breed that gives very creamy milk and makes an ideal "family" cow. Finn and Normande are two other breeds.

Milk is a high-quality food, rich in protein, fats, and essential minerals. Through selective breeding, agricultural scientists have recently improved both the quantity and quality of milk produced. Compared with her counterpart of 40 years ago, the modern dairy cow produces over twice as much milk, with a higher fat content.

The best-quality milk is generally used for butter and cheese making. These milk products are a much more concentrated form of food, and are more easily stored than fresh milk, which goes sour very quickly.

Great Britain makes more use of fresh milk than any other country. Nearly 70 percent of its total milk production is consumed in this way. By contrast, less than 10 percent of New Zealand's milk is drunk as a liquid; most is turned into butter for export. In the developed countries as a whole, about 15 percent of production is made into cheese.

Finn

Jersey

Normande

Brown Swiss

► A modern circular milking parlor in Scotland. The cattle are milked by sophisticated equipment while they stand on a rotating platform. The farmer can adjust the time of rotation to the average length of milking. This arrangement is expensive but very efficient because it permits a steady flow of cattle through the parlor. Only one operator is needed.

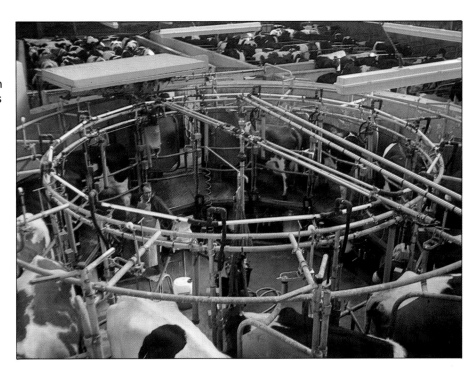

Milk from each species, 1988

(in million metric tons)

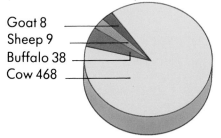

Goat 8
Sheep 9
Buffalo 38
Cow 468

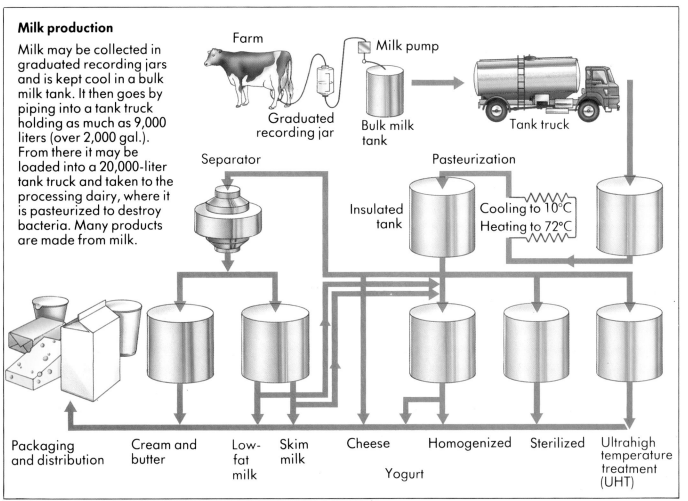

Milk production

Milk may be collected in graduated recording jars and is kept cool in a bulk milk tank. It then goes by piping into a tank truck holding as much as 9,000 liters (over 2,000 gal.). From there it may be loaded into a 20,000-liter tank truck and taken to the processing dairy, where it is pasteurized to destroy bacteria. Many products are made from milk.

Farm

Milk pump

Graduated recording jar

Bulk milk tank

Tank truck

Separator

Pasteurization

Insulated tank

Cooling to 10°C
Heating to 72°C

Packaging and distribution

Cream and butter

Low-fat milk

Skim milk

Cheese

Yogurt

Homogenized

Sterilized

Ultrahigh temperature treatment (UHT)

Beef cattle

Beef and veal are the most expensive forms of meat to produce, yet they are so popular that they account for one-third of world meat consumption. The taste for beef is concentrated in the developed world. In most other regions cattle are too valuable to be killed for food.

Cattle are not particularly efficient meat producers, and only about 60 percent of the animal is edible. Beef cattle require high-quality food in order to put on weight, and in Europe and North America they are raised almost entirely on concentrated feeds.

In the developed world, only beef from cattle that have been fed on grain or oilseed "cake" is considered fit for the table. Meat from cattle that have been ranched on grassland is generally of lower quality and is only used in hamburgers and processed meat products.

European breeds produce the best-quality meat, but cannot tolerate warm climates or poor grazing. The huge herds that are now ranched in South and Central America are largely composed of longhorn and zebu cattle that have been improved by crossbreeding with European stock.

In parts of the United States and Europe, beef cattle are now raised very intensively, and some animals, especially those destined for veal, spend their whole life indoors.

▶ Modern beef cattle are not as sturdily built as the ancient aurochs, but some of them approach it. The Hereford is the main British meat producer, and has also been crossbred with American stock. The Simmental and Blue Belgian breeds both achieve great size and reflect attempts to produce the most meat possible.

▶ (opposite) Welsh Black cattle are smaller than most beef cattle. Being strong and sturdy, they are well suited to their native upland terrain.

Aurochs

Hereford

Simmental

Blue Belgian

Other livestock

Spot facts

• The heaviest hog ever recorded was in Tennessee in 1933. The animal weighed 1,158 kg (2,552 lb.) and measured 2.7 m (9 ft.) long.

• The heaviest fleece from a sheep weighed 24.5 kg (54 lb.) and was taken from an Australian Merino that had not been sheared for five years.

• The world's largest chicken farm, in Ohio, produces 3.7 million eggs per day.

• There are about 15 billion domestic animals (3 for every person), most of them birds.

• The largest chicken egg ever recorded was laid in 1896 and weighed nearly 340 g (12 oz.).

▶ The nomadic peoples of southern Central Asia and Mongolia obtain meat, milk, and clothing from their flocks of goats. During a year, the flocks may be herded hundreds of kilometers between summer and winter pasture. In mountainous regions, the flocks are brought down to the valleys for the winter, to avoid the worst weather.

Very few other animal species are important in world agriculture. Pigs are the most efficient meat producers, and it was the boast of some American meat packers that no part of a pig was wasted.

In general, sheep and goats are the most versatile livestock, providing meat, milk, and wool. Goats are also extremely hardy and are found in mountain ranges and on the fringes of deserts.

Poultry have long been a source of meat and eggs. During the twentieth century, poultry farming has become a huge industry in the developed world. In terms of increasing productivity, chicken is the fastest growing foodstuff in the world.

In many parts of the developing world, horses, mules, donkeys, camels, and, in South America, llamas all have a limited role in agriculture.

Pigs

Wild pigs are found in many parts of the world, and their domesticated cousins are the world's major meat producers. Each year, a world population of over 800 million pigs produces over 60 million metric tons of meat. With the best breeds, up to 80 percent of the animal can be turned into food.

Pigs are natural scavengers; they will eat almost anything and need little attention. In Asia, many families buy one or two piglets each year to fatten up on kitchen scraps. In Europe and North America, which have about half the world's pigs, most of the animals are reared intensively and indoors. Where possible, many farmers fatten their pigs on seasonal fruits such as acorns.

Pigs are well suited to mass-production methods, and modern farmers aim to get at least 20 piglets per breeding female per year. When fed on grains and protein supplements, each piglet will grow about 65 kg (140 lb.) of usable meat in just six months.

Pig meat deteriorates rapidly in hot climates, and some cultures consider it unclean. In cooler climates, pork is ideally suited to traditional forms of preservation, such as smoking and salting, to produce ham and bacon. Large, solidly built breeds are often referred to as "bacon-type" hogs. Other traditional breeds, often known as the "lard-type" breeds, were raised to produce meat with a lot of fat. Chinese pigs also produce fatty meat. In the developed world, public taste now favours lean meat from leaner pigs such as the Landrace.

Meat from different animals, 1988 (million metric tons per year)

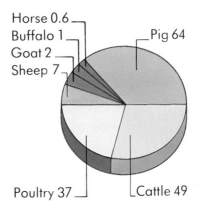

Horse 0.6
Buffalo 1
Goat 2
Sheep 7
Pig 64
Poultry 37
Cattle 49

◀ The pig is the world's number one meat producer, accounting for about 40 percent of the total annual production of over 160 million tons. Cattle are the next most important (30 percent), followed by poultry (23 percent). All other types of meat together make up the rest.

1 Landrace
2 Duroc
3 Berkshire
4 Andalusian
5 Craon

▲ (1) Landrace pig from Denmark, a lean pig that has recently increased in popularity. Traditional European breeds such as (2) Duroc, (3) Berkshire, (4) Andalusian, and (5) Craon were bred to be hugely fat, and are now less popular.

Sheep

The sheep is a multipurpose animal that provides meat, milk, and wool. Sheep are raised throughout the world, and have the greatest commercial importance in Australasia, Europe, and Argentina. In New Zealand, for example, sheep outnumber people by a ratio of 20 to 1. In Great Britain, 90 percent of sheep are raised for meat, nearly all of it in the form of lamb. In other countries, milk for yogurt and cheese making and wool are the major products.

Sheep are hardy animals that perform well on a diet of grass, and may be kept outdoors all year round. Their heavy woolen fleece is naturally waterproof, and provides excellent insulation. Apart from shearing and the lambing season, sheep do not require much attention. A flock of 500 may be tended by a single shepherd and a dog. Having a thick fleece makes sheep very attractive to ticks and other parasites. Most developed countries require their sheep to be dipped regularly in pesticides. Sheep that have been dipped are marked with a brightly colored dye.

There are hundreds of different varieties of sheep that have been bred to take advantage of different types of grazing. In general, upland sheep are closer to the domestic sheep's primitive ancestors. Upland breeds provide less wool and meat per animal, but will graze on windswept hillsides that are too cold and exposed for their more refined downland cousins. Downland sheep require more attention, but are well suited to the production of quick-growing lambs for meat.

There are many local breeds of long-wool sheep, but the world's dominant wool producer is the Merino. The breed originated in Spain, and was taken by colonists to South America, South Africa, and Australasia. By 1900, Australia had over 100 million sheep, virtually all of them Merinos. The Merino, and breeds developed from it, is widespread in the United States. Sheep are second only to cattle as a source of animal products. World output of sheep products each year includes 9 million metric tons of milk and 7 million of meat.

▶ Long-wool sheep on a French mountainside.

▼ (1) Sudanese sheep. The Merino has been crossbred with many local sheep, (2) is the Arles variety. (3) The West African dwarf breed inhabits the humid forest zone, and the Soay (4) lives in the Outer Hebrides.

1 Sudanese

3 West African dwarf

2 Arles

4 Soay

Sheepshearing is hard and very skilled work. Fleeces can weigh as much as 12 kg (26 lb.) each, and the huge size of some flocks (up to 50,000 animals) means that each shearer has to deal with 40-50 animals per hour. Scientists are now working on producing a sheep that would shed its fleece after a single injection of hormones.

Goats

Goats are closely related to sheep, and are agile and hardy animals. The more primitive breeds of both species closely resemble each other, and in the warmer parts of the world they are often raised in mixed flocks. Like sheep, goats provide highly nutritious milk that is often made into cheese. Goats are also important for wool and leather. In total the world has over 500 million domestic goats. Over 2 million metric tons of goat meat are produced each year, over 8 million metric tons of goat milk, and over 400,000 metric tons of fresh goatskins.

In general, goats can thrive in a more arid climate, and on lower-quality grazing, than sheep. In this respect they are extremely useful because they can take advantage of land that would otherwise be useless for agriculture. But goats can also be very destructive.

A combination of agility and wide-ranging appetite means that without careful management, goats will devour all the available vegetation, which in turn encourages soil erosion. They are usually kept tethered.

Some breeds of goat tolerate the cold better than other domestic animals, and mountain peoples often rely entirely on goats for both food and clothing. Some Asian breeds are especially noted for their high quality wool. Cashmere is obtained from a breed of goat originally from northern India. Each goat provides only up to half a kilogram (1 lb.) of fibers a year. Mohair is the hair of the Angora goat, originally from central Turkey. Both breeds are now farmed.

In Europe and North America, goats are kept for milk production and are often raised intensively on concentrated feeds. The Swiss goat is the traditional milking breed, although during this century it has been challenged by a hybrid strain, called the Nubian in the United States. This goat is actually a cross between the small English goat and a larger Egyptian breed. Known in England as the Anglo-Nubian, this cross was first introduced around 1900. By 1950, half of all goats raised in the United States were Nubians. In Europe, the Swiss goat remains dominant.

► The agility of goats is legendary. Goats appearing to climb trees are a familiar sight in warm countries.

▼ The commercial production of goat's milk can be mechanized in the same way as that of cow's milk.

74

Nordic

Nubian

Saanen

▶ Breeds raised for milk production include: Nordic, from northern Scandinavia; Nubian (Anglo-Nubian), a common sight in North America; French Alpine, which is found in most parts of France, Saanen, originally from Switzerland and now farmed all over the world; British Alpine, a cross between English and Swiss breeds; Mamber, from the Syrian mountains, a typical Middle Eastern breed; and Murcia-Granada, which is found only in southern Spain.

French Alpine

British Alpine

Mamber

Murcia-Granada

Poultry

Chickens dominate the world's poultry population; over 90 percent of all farmed birds are chickens. In the Western world, chicken is becoming the most popular form of meat. In 1950 Great Britain consumed less than 5 million chickens. Forty years later, the total has increased to 500 million, and is predicted to reach 1 billion by the year 2000. Each year the world consumes over 30 million metric tons of poultry meat, and an equivalent weight of eggs.

In the developed world, laying hens and those destined for meat (broilers) are usually raised intensively. The birds are kept in large buildings containing thousands of individual cages arranged in stacks (batteries). They are fed carefully controlled amounts of food by a conveyor-belt system. By the use of artificial lighting, the hens' natural egg-laying cycle can be altered so that they provide a constant supply of eggs.

In Britain and the United States, turkeys are raised intensively for seasonal consumption, but are slowly becoming a year-round food. Geese, however, are declining in popularity. In Asia, ducks are often raised on flooded rice paddies. Duck meat and eggs are used.

▲ Turkeys in Wisconsin being fattened on expensive grain for the Thanksgiving table. The mass-production of poultry demands very large numbers of birds, and turkeys are not suitable for confinement in batteries. Open-air raising brings risks of injuries from fighting.

◄ Ducks on the Pacific island of Bali being driven to market. Ducks are one of the most widespread bird families, and throughout the world local species have been domesticated for egg and meat production. They require little attention, but do need a pond.

► Chicks hatching in an incubator. Efficient poultry production requires control over every stage of the process. An incubator permits the eggs to hatch under the most ideal artificial conditions, thus ensuring that the greatest possible number of chicks survive.

◄ Toulouse geese are among the largest domesticated birds.

▼ Birds outnumber mammals two to one. Each farm mammal yields about 30 kg (nearly 70 lb.) of meat per year, and each bird less than 7 kg (14 lb.) of protein, half as eggs.

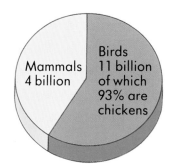

Mammals 4 billion

Birds 11 billion of which 93% are chickens

Mammals meat 127 million metric tons

Birds meat 37 eggs 35 million metric tons.

Fishing

Spot facts

● Between 1964 and 1975, the catch of North Atlantic haddock fell by more than 90 percent as a result of fishing methods that were too efficient.

● A modern factory ship can process over 1,000 metric tons of fish per day, and may remain at sea for up to nine months.

● One-third of all the fish caught off the West African coast are used as fertilizer and animal feed in the developed countries of the world.

● A Chinese fish farm can produce 4.5 metric tons of animal protein per hectare (about 1.8 per acre) per year, 10 times more than if the same area of land were used for mammal livestock.

▶ Fish caught in a trawl net being hauled aboard a side trawler. Harvesting the sea is now as mechanized as harvesting the land. But in agricultural terms, our approach to the oceans is still primitive. The crop of wild fish is steadily declining in the face of overfishing. More and more of the fish we eat comes from fish farms.

Fishing represents the only significant source of human food that still relies on natural food chains. Our attitude to the sea is still largely that of the hunter-gatherer.

On average, the world gets about 6 percent of its protein from fish and shellfish, but in some countries, including Japan, Southeast Asia, Portugal, Norway, the Soviet Union, and some West African countries, the proportion is considerably greater. About a third of the total marine catch is not used as human food, but is converted into animal feed and fertilizer.

Modern fishing methods are extremely efficient, and overfishing is now the industry's greatest problem. Part of the response has been a revival of fish-farming.

Fishing grounds

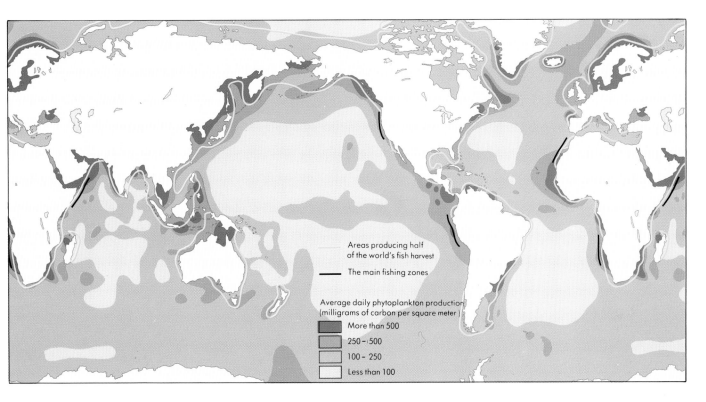

Areas producing half
of the world's fish harvest

—— The main fishing zones

Average daily phytoplankton production
(milligrams of carbon per square meter)

■	More than 500
■	250 – 500
□	100 – 250
□	Less than 100

▲ Microscopic phytoplankton produce food from sunlight using photosynthesis. Marine scientists can calculate the food content of seawater by measuring the quantity of carbon in the phytoplankton.

▼ Tiny shrimplike krill occur in great numbers in the oceans around Antarctica. The Soviet Union catches about 1 million metric tons per year.

Most of the fish we eat stand fairly high in the ocean food chains. They occur in the greatest numbers in coastal waters, where plant life is most abundant. It is warmer here, and there is a runoff of nutrients from the land.

Offshore fish populations are concentrated in fairly shallow waters less than 150 m (500 ft.) above the continental shelf, where concentrations of phytoplankton are greatest. The richest fishing grounds are often associated with the upwelling of deep ocean currents that carry nutrient-rich waters from mid-ocean.

One of the world's most productive fishing grounds, off the coast of Peru, was fed by the El Niño current that brought plankton from the central Pacific. During the early 1970s, the Peruvian fishing industry landed over 13 million metric tons of fish per year. A sudden change of direction in the current deprived the area of most of its food supply. Within ten years, catches had dropped to less than 2 million metric tons of fish per year.

Catching the fish

The richest fishing grounds within easy reach are coastal shallows, lagoons, and river estuaries. Some rivers are used by migratory fish, such as the salmon, and provide an additional seasonal harvest. Many shellfish, for example shrimps, are also plentiful during the spawning season and can be collected with little effort.

Shallow waters, up to 15 m (50 ft.) deep, can be fished from small boats powered by oars or paddles. A wide variety of methods are still used for subsistence fishing. Nets, baited hooks, spears, even trained seabirds such as cormorants, are employed to catch fish. But only large nets, handled by many fishermen working together, are capable of landing a worthwhile surplus which can be sold.

Most commercial fishing takes place offshore, where pelagic and demersal fish account for over 75 percent of the total catch. Pelagic fish include herring, sardines, and tuna; they occur in free-swimming schools at depths up to 150 m (500 ft.). Demersal fish, such as cod and plaice, are bottom-dwellers found on the continental shelf and offshore banks.

In recent years the world commercial fish catch has exceeded 90 million metric tons annually. Some 60 percent of the total is landed by just 10 countries, with Japan and the Soviet Union each taking more than 10 percent.

World fish production has risen since the mid-1980s, largely thanks to fish-farming output. The catch had been static for years despite increased use of modern fishing fleets and factory ships that can process the catch in mid-ocean. Populations of traditional food fish have been falling because of overfishing. Switching to other species, many used only for animal feed and fertilizer, has helped maintain the volume of the catch.

Pollution has also affected the quality of the catch. Some important species have been found to have acquired dangerous levels of poisonous pollutants through bioconcentration.

▶ Shore fishermen in Malaysia. One major disadvantage of shore fishing with a net, is that large fish are fairly rare. The average size of the fish caught is usually very small: less than 15 cm (6 in.).

▼ These are important species of commercial marine fish. These species swim well clear of the seabed and are found in wide ranges of seas. The limits of their territory are set by the temperature of the water.

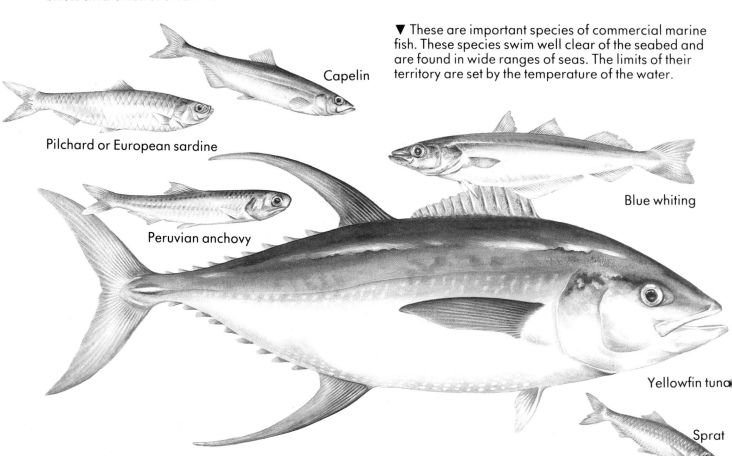

Capelin

Pilchard or European sardine

Peruvian anchovy

Blue whiting

Yellowfin tuna

Sprat

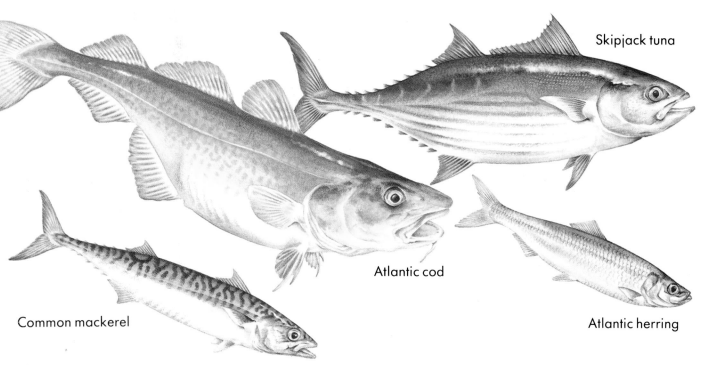

Skipjack tuna

Atlantic cod

Common mackerel

Atlantic herring

Netting methods

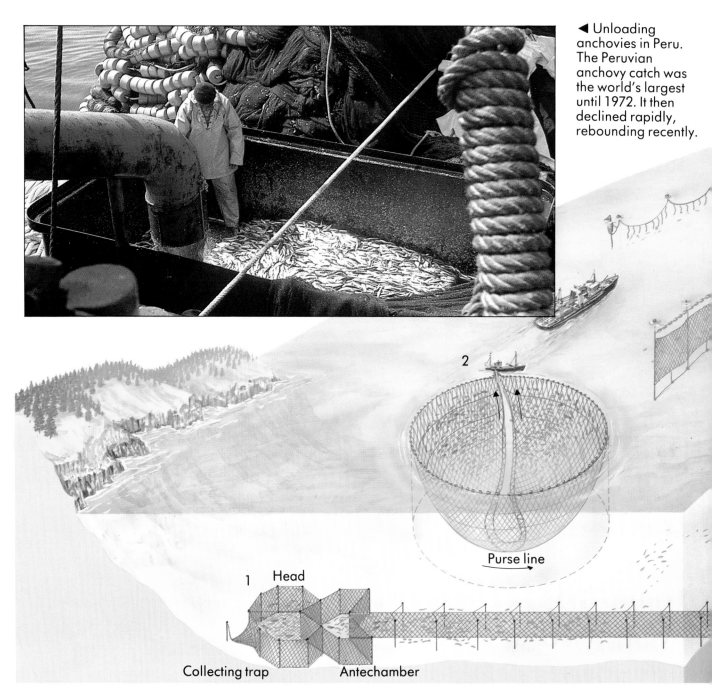

◄ Unloading anchovies in Peru. The Peruvian anchovy catch was the world's largest until 1972. It then declined rapidly, rebounding recently.

2

Purse line

1 Head

Collecting trap

Antechamber

Top twenty fish in a recent year

A fairly small number of species dominate the sea's harvest. The Alaska pollack and the Japanese pilchard (a type of sardine) together make up over 10 percent of today's catch. Some commercially important species are completely unknown to most people. For example, the Gulf menhaden, which makes up 15 percent of the United States' catch, is not considered fit for human consumption. Much of the catch of menhaden is processed into animal feed.

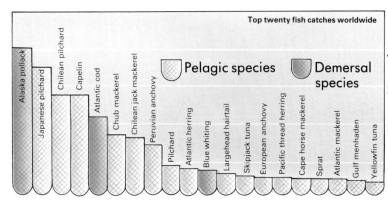

Top twenty fish catches worldwide

Alaska pollack
Japanese pilchard
Chilean pilchard
Capelin
Atlantic cod
Chub mackerel
Chilean jack mackerel
Peruvian anchovy
Pilchard
Atlantic herring
Blue whiting
Largehead hairtail
Skipjack tuna
European anchovy
Pacific thread herring
Cape horse mackerel
Sprat
Atlantic mackerel
Gulf menhaden
Yellowfin tuna

Pelagic species   Demersal species

Million metric tons
4
3
2
1

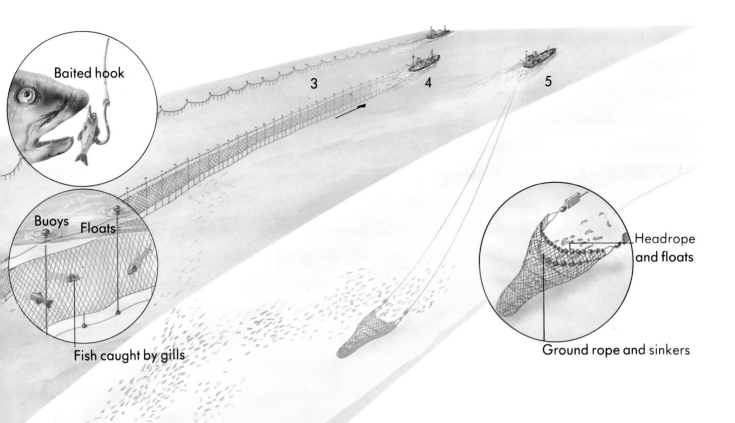

Baited hook

Buoys Floats

Fish caught by gills

Headrope and floats

Ground rope and sinkers

3 4 5

▲ (1) Fixed net (2) Seining (3) Long-lining (4) Drifting (5) Trawling. Overfishing is not only a matter of simply taking too many fish. In all forms of net fishing, the size of the individuals caught can be controlled by varying the size of the mesh in the net. Taking too many small (young) fish causes the population as a whole to decline.

The basic technology of fishing is very simple, and the vast majority of fish are caught in nets from boats. Other methods, such as netting fish from the beach or trapping shellfish in baskets, have only local importance. In some estuaries and straits, complex arrangements of fixed nets are employed to lead fish into a fixed collecting trap, which is regularly emptied.

Trawling and seining are the two most important sea-fishing techniques. Today, the fish are actively pursued, often by means of echolocation equipment. A trawl net may be drawn by one or two ships. If a single ship is used, "otter boards" are employed to keep the mouth of the net open. Both pelagic and demersal fish are caught by trawling.

A seine is a single net that is drawn around a school of pelagic fish like a purse. Some seine nets are over 1,000 m (3,000 ft.) long. Seining was developed from drifting, in which a net is merely trailed behind a slowly moving boat. Floats and weights are fitted to the net to keep it upright in the water.

Some fish, especially cod, are caught on a commercial scale on hooks. Trailed from a fishing ship, a single longline might hold 5,000 individually baited hooks.

Farming the waters

▶ An inland fish farm in Arizona. Linking the ponds allows a flow of clean water from one to another.

▼ A French oyster farm at low tide. When the tide comes in, the shellfish can feed on nutrients in the water.

▼ These are some of the more widely cultivated vertebrate fish. Catfish are bottom-feeding scavengers, and carp are herbivorous. Herbivorous species can be fed more cheaply than carnivores and tend to be more highly productive. They need little management.

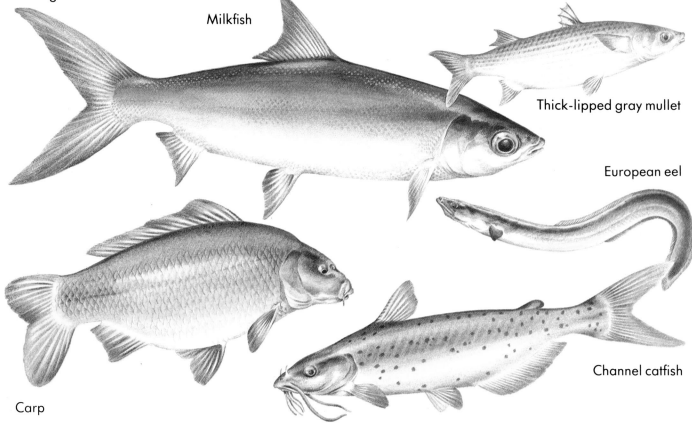

Milkfish

Thick-lipped gray mullet

European eel

Channel catfish

Carp

Fish-farming, the breeding and raising fish like farm animals, is a continuing tradition in much of Asia. The technique has achieved its highest sophistication in China, where a freshwater fish pond can produce 10 times as much protein as the same amount of farmland.

A Chinese fish pond is a complete ecosystem in which all the species are edible. The upper and middle levels of the pond are occupied by various species of carp. Their diet of water plants and algae is supplemented by waste vegetation. At the bottom of the pond, dace feed on the detritus and keep the water clean. Fish are also raised in flooded paddy fields, and are shifted from one field to another when the time comes for rice planting and harvest.

Throughout the Pacific, especially in Indonesia, thousands of hectares of coastal mangrove swamps are farmed for marine species. Milkfish and groupers are raised in large ponds, and shrimp are harvested regularly like crops.

In other parts of the world, the traditional fish ponds fell into disuse centuries ago. Until very recently, fish-farming has been confined to some shellfish such as oysters and lobsters.

During the last 20 years there has been a tremendous revival in fish-farming, especially in the United States and Europe. One quarter of British fish consumption now consists of trout and salmon produced on farms. Trout are raised in ponds or enclosed stretches of river. Salmon are farmed in estuaries and sea lochs in Scotland. The fish are contained within huge floating cages as large as a football field. A single farm may have over 500,000 live fish at various stages of growth. All the food for both salmon and trout has to be provided by the farmer.

Fish kept in enclosed conditions are extremely vulnerable to attack from disease and parasites. Fish farmers in Western countries use large quantities of powerful pesticides to protect their fish. There is mounting concern about such substances being released directly into marine ecosystems.

▼ Netting salmon at a saltwater fish farm in Washington State. After harvest, the first task is to remove eggs which are used for raising the next generation. Young salmon are initially raised in fresh water, as in nature.

Units of measurement

Units of measurement

This encyclopedia gives measurements in metric units, which are commonly used in science. Approximate equivalents in traditional American units, sometimes called U.S. customary units, are also given in the text, in parentheses.

Some common metric and U.S. units

Here are some equivalents, accurate to parts per million. For many practical purposes rougher equivalents may be adequate, especially when the quantity being converted from one system to the other is known with an accuracy of just one or two digits. Equivalents marked with an asterisk (*) are exact.

Volume
1 cubic centimeter = 0.0610237 cubic inch
1 cubic meter = 35.3147 cubic feet
1 cubic meter = 1.30795 cubic yards
1 cubic kilometer = 0.239913 cubic mile

1 cubic inch = 16.3871 cubic centimeters
1 cubic foot = 0.0283168 cubic meter
1 cubic yard = 0.764555 cubic meter

Liquid measure
1 milliliter = 0.0338140 fluidounce
1 liter = 1.05669 quarts

1 fluidounce = 29.5735 milliliters
1 quart = 0.946353 liter

Mass and weight
1 gram = 0.0352740 ounce
1 kilogram = 2.20462 pounds
1 metric ton = 1.10231 short tons

1 ounce = 28.3495 grams
1 pound = 0.453592 kilogram
1 short ton = 0.907185 metric ton

Length
1 millimeter = 0.0393701 inch
1 centimeter = 0.393701 inch
1 meter = 3.28084 feet
1 meter = 1.09361 yards
1 kilometer = 0.621371 mile

1 inch = 2.54* centimeters
1 foot = 0.3048* meter
1 yard = 0.9144* meter
1 mile = 1.60934 kilometers

Area
1 square centimeter = 0.155000 square inch
1 square meter = 10.7639 square feet
1 square meter = 1.19599 square yards
1 square kilometer = 0.386102 square mile

1 square inch = 6.4516* square centimeters
1 square foot = 0.0929030 square meter
1 square yard = 0.836127 square meter
1 square mile = 2.58999 square kilometers

1 hectare = 2.47105 acres
1 acre = 0.404686 hectare

Temperature conversions

To convert temperatures in degrees Celsius to temperatures in degrees Fahrenheit, or vice versa, use these formulas:

Celsius Temperature = (Fahrenheit Temperature − 32) × 5/9
Fahrenheit Temperature = (Celsius Temperature × 9/5) + 32

Numbers and abbreviations

Numbers

Scientific measurements sometimes involve extremely large numbers. Scientists often express large numbers in a concise "exponential" form using powers of 10. The number one billion, or 1,000,000,000, if written in this form, would be 10^9; three billion, or 3,000,000,000, would be 3×10^9. The "exponent" 9 tells you that there are nine zeros following the 3. More complicated numbers can be written in this way by using decimals; for example, 3.756×10^9 is the same as 3,756,000,000.

Very small numbers – numbers close to zero – can be written in exponential form with a minus sign on the exponent. For example, one-billionth, which is 1/1,000,000,000 or 0.000000001, would be 10^{-9}. Here, the 9 in the exponent -9 tells you that, in the decimal form of the number, the 1 is in the ninth place to the right of the decimal point. Three-billionths, or 3/1,000,000,000, would be 3×10^{-9}; accordingly, 3.756×10^{-9} would mean 0.000000003756 (or 3.756/1,000,000,000).

Here are the American names of some powers of ten, and how they are written in numerals:

1 million (10^6)	1,000,000
1 billion (10^9)	1,000,000,000
1 trillion (10^{12})	1,000,000,000,000
1 quadrillion (10^{15})	1,000,000,000,000,000
1 quintillion (10^{18})	1,000,000,000,000,000,000
1 sextillion (10^{21})	1,000,000,000,000,000,000,000
1 septillion (10^{24})	1,000,000,000,000,000,000,000,000

Principal abbreviations used in the encyclopedia

°C	degrees Celsius	kg	kilogram
cc	cubic centimeter	l	liter
cm	centimeter	lb.	pound
cu.	cubic	m	meter
d	days	mi.	mile
°F	degrees Fahrenheit	ml	milliliter
fl. oz.	fluidounce	mm	millimeter
fps	feet per second	mph	miles per hour
ft.	foot	mps	miles per second
g	gram	mya	millions of years ago
h	hour	N	north
Hz	hertz	oz.	ounce
in.	inch	qt.	quart
K	kelvin (degree temperature)	s	second
		S	south
		sq.	square
		V	volt
		y	year
		yd.	yard

Glossary

acid rain Rainwater containing pollutants that chemically attack stone and trees. It can rapidly make a river or lake completely lifeless.

adaptation Process by which the characteristics of a species gradually change in response to the environment. The term can also refer to a particular characteristic.

agave Group of subtropical plants that are cultivated for the fibers produced in the leaves.

Angora Breed of goat from central Turkey that produces the fibers known as mohair.

artificial insemination Introduction of sperm into a female animal by mechanical methods, usually with a syringe. The technique enables a bull to breed with cows all over the world.

bacteria Group of microorganisms that are neither plants nor animals. They are the smallest and most primitive form of life. A few species cause disease in humans and are a major pest.

battery Row of poultry cages arranged in multistory stacks. In the developed world, most chickens are raised in batteries.

bioconcentration Process by which a pollutant is retained inside animal bodies, and becomes more concentrated as it moves up a food chain.

boll Tangle of white fibers that forms around the seeds of the cotton plant. The most notorious pest of cotton is the boll weevil.

broiler Chicken raised to be eaten as meat.

burlap Material woven from the fibers obtained from the jute or hemp plants.

calorie Unit for measuring quantity of heat; used to indicate the energy value of foods. Carbohydrates, oils, and fats contain the most calories.

canopy Layer of dense foliage that forms the roof of a rain forest about 30 m (100 ft) above the ground. It is the most densely populated part of the forest.

carbon dioxide Gas present in Earth's atmosphere that is essential to many of the processes of life. Increased levels of carbon dioxide, caused by pollution and habitat destruction, are slowly causing our planet to get warmer.

carnivore Animal that feeds on other animals; a meat eater.

cash crop Any crop, food or otherwise, that is grown for sale rather than for consumption by the farmer.

cashmere Breed of goat from northern India that produces the very high-quality fibers of the same name.

cereal Any of the grain-producing plants that are cultivated for food. Wheat, rice, maize (corn), barley, oats, rye, and sorghum are the most important cereals.

CFCs Chlorofluorocarbons, a group of gases that are believed to be causing considerable damage to the Earth's ozone layer.

climax community End product of the process of succession; a community composed of long-established populations living in a natural balance with each other.

colonists Species that have adaptations that enable them to establish themselves on any unoccupied land that becomes available.

combustion products Fumes and minute particles released into the atmosphere during the process of combustion (burning.)

community All the plants and animals that exist within a shared habitat. Communities are the building blocks from which ecosystems are constructed.

cross-fertilization Technique used in plant breeding. The plants are carefully protected from any pollen in the atmosphere, and each plant is individually pollinated by hand.

demersal Describes bottom-dwelling fish.

detritus Silt and sediment that usually contain dead and decaying organic matter.

domestication Gradual process by which certain plants and animals became tamed and shaped by human beings. Over many centuries, domesticated species have become very different from their wild relatives.

draft animal Any livestock which is kept primarily for animal-power, usually pulling a plow.

ecology Study of the relationships between living organisms and their environment. Ecologists look at the big picture, the way species behave toward each other.

ecosphere Planet Earth. Our planet is the only object in the Universe on which we know life exists. We have only one ecosphere available for study.

ecosystem Network of relationships between living organisms in a particular location. An ecosystem can be as small as an individual field, or as large as an ocean.

endangered Describes a species that because of decreasing population or shrinking habitat (or a combination of both), is likely to become extinct in the wild unless it is carefully protected.

environment All physical conditions, e.g. land surface (or type of water), climate, atmosphere, and other life forms, that together form the normal surroundings for a particular species.

eutrophication Process by which the oxygen in a body of water becomes used up by the decaying bodies of microorganisms that were stimulated into overgrowth by an abundance of nutrients. A common result of nitrate pollution.

evolution The generally accepted theory that life began with very simple forms that have gradually developed into more complex forms.

extensive Describes any form of agriculture that requires large areas of land, and a crop that largely looks after itself, e.g. cattle ranching or olive groves.

fallout Fine dust of radioactive particles produced by the explosion of a nuclear device on the Earth's surface, or in the atmosphere.

fertilization The first stage of sexual reproduction, in which a male sex cell and a female sex cell join together to form a single cell that will develop into a new individual.

fertilizer Any substance added to soil in order to increase the amount of nutrients available for crops. Natural fertilizers include compost, animal manure, and fish meal. Artificial fertilizers are now manufactured by the chemical industry.

flax Flowering plant found in cool, damp climates; fibers from the stem are used to make linen.

food chain Process by which many animals that eat food in turn become food for others, e.g. cows eat grass, people eat cows. Food chains indicate a flow of energy through an ecosystem toward the top predators.

food web Map of the movement of food (energy) through an ecosystem. Food webs are usually pyramid-shaped, with predators at the top.

free range Method of raising poultry or other animals in which the animals largely fend for themselves, with only limited additional feed and nighttime shelter.

fungi Group of organisms, including mushrooms and molds, that share a few of the characteristics of primitive plants, but which do not photosynthesize.

game preserve Protected area within which wildlife can enjoy an almost natural existence. Also called a game or wildlife refuge, reserve, or sanctuary.

genetic engineering Collective term for the various techniques that have been discovered which enable scientists to manipulate DNA and produce characteristics which do not occur in nature.

ginning Process of combing the seeds out of a cotton boll so that the fibers can be used to make cloth.

glaciation Process by which the land surface is smoothed and shaped by the action of glaciers, rivers of ice that move very slowly. Today, glaciers are confined to mountainous regions and the poles.

Green movement Unofficial alliance of many different pressure groups who are concerned with various environmental and ecological issues such as preserving habitats and wildlife and preventing pollution.

Green Revolution Usually refers to the introduction of hybrid cereals to the developing world after 1960. In a more general sense it applies to all the advances in agriculture since World War 2.

greenhouse effect Gradual warming of the Earth's atmosphere due to pollution, mainly in the form of carbon dioxide.

habitat Natural surroundings in which a particular plant or animal exists. The term is much more specific and localized than "environment."

herbivore Animal that feeds exclusively on plants.

hormones Chemical messengers used to carry instructions around the bodies of organisms.

hunter-gatherer Primitive life-style that predates agriculture, but which still occurs in isolated parts of Asia, Africa, and South America. In general, the males hunt and the females gather nuts, fruit, and roots.

hybrid Result of breeding between two different varieties of the same species. Although individual hybrids often occur in nature, hybrid strains are usually the result of human intervention.

incubator Equipment used to provide constant temperatures for the hatching of eggs or the care of young birds and animals.

Industrial Revolution Period of rapid industrial development that began in Great Britain during the 1700s, characterized by a massive increase in the use of coal as a fuel.

intensive Describes any form of agriculture that employs special techniques to obtain greater productivity from the land. The most extreme form is factory farming.

irrigation Provision of additional water for crops. Flooding is the simplest method, and the first dams were built over 5,000 years ago. Today, many different methods are used to provide extra water.

jute Tropical plant that produces strong fibers in its stem that are used to make sacking and ropes.

kapok Short, fluffy fibers obtained from the seeds of a tropical tree. Formerly, kapok was widely used for insulation and quilted jackets.

krill Tiny shrimp found in huge numbers in the waters around Antarctica. Many scientists believe they represent a key source of food for the future.

legume Edible seed of plants such as peas, beans, and lentils. The term is often used to refer to this group of plants, rather than the food they produce.

linseed oil High-quality oil, obtained from the seeds of the flax plant; it is used mainly in the paint and polish industries.

malnutrition General term for any bodily disorder caused by a defective diet. Deficiencies of particular vitamins cause particular illnesses, and general undernourishment creates weak and sickly people who generally have a short life expectancy.

mangrove Tropical tree that grows in shallow water and swamps, and which creates a distinctive and productive ecosystem.

Merino Breed of sheep famous for producing large amounts of high-quality wool.

mixed farming Type of agriculture that originated in northern Europe, and which combines the growing of wheat alongside cattle and a variety of other crops.

molasses Thick brown liquid, a stage in the production of sugar from sugarcane.

monoculture Cultivation of the same crop over very large areas of land. Producing enough staple crops to feed the world would be impossible without monoculture.

national park Area of land within which building or development is generally not permitted, and the wildlife is protected.

niche Position of a species within an ecosystem, defined by the space the species occupies, and by its feeding activity.

nitrate Chemical compound containing the element nitrogen. It is one of the main ingredients of artificial fertilizers.

nomads People who have no fixed settlements, but who are constantly on the move. Such peoples are usually animal herders, and their life-style is dictated by the seasonal availability of grazing.

nuclear Relating to the nucleus, or central part, of an atom. Nuclear energy is the energy produced when atoms, particularly uranium atoms, split.

omnivore Animal that feeds on both plant and vegetable matter. Omniverous species, e.g. humans, rats, cockroaches, are among the most successful.

organic farming Any method of cultivating food that does not involve the use of chemical additives, such as artificial fertilizers.

ozone Form of oxygen gas, the "tang" in sea air. A layer of ozone in the atmosphere filters out most of the harmful effects of the Sun's ultraviolet rays.

paddy Small field surrounded by low banks, and used for rice cultivation. Rice has to remain submerged for 75 percent of its growing period, and paddies are flooded for much of the year.

parasites Organisms that obtain nourishment by feeding directly off the body systems of others. Livestock are liable to infestation with both external parasites (ticks and fleas) and internal parasites (flukes and worms).

pelagic Describes fish that occur in free-swimming shoals in water up to 150 m (500 ft) deep.

pest Any species that, through its own existence, endangers human beings. Weeds, some insects and animals, and many species of fungi and microorganisms are all pests.

pesticide Any substance that kills pests. Some pesticides use natural ingredients, but most contain deadly poisonous chemicals which can become concentrated by natural food chains.

phosphate Chemical compound containing the element phosphorus. It is one of the main ingredients of artificial fertilizers.

photosynthesis Process by which plants manufacture food from water, carbon dioxide, and sunlight.

phytoplankton Tiny single-celled plants that through photosynthesis provide the basis for the oceans' food web.

plankton Tiny, single-celled plants and animals that live in both salt and fresh water. Plant plankton, also known as phytoplankton, forms the basis for most of the ocean's food web, and, like land plants, removes carbon dioxide from the atmosphere.

plantation Type of farm, usually occurring in tropical climates, that is devoted to the intensive cultivation of a single high-value crop, e.g. tea, rubber, or sugarcane.

pollen Tiny grains produced by flowers that contain the plant's male sex cells.

pollutant Any substance that is present in the environment in unnatural quantities, whether it is directly harmful or not.

pollution Introduction and distribution of unnatural amounts of dangerous substances into the land, water, and air that form our environment.

population All the members of a particular species that exist within a defined area. In nature, populations rise and fall in relation to the availability of food.

predator Any animal that actively hunts other animals (known as prey for food. Most carnivores are also predators.

primary consumers Animals that feed on plants (primary producers).

primary producers Plants, so-called because of the role they play in food webs, producing food by photosynthesis.

radiation Means by which energy travels through empty space or a gas, e.g. the atmosphere. The term is widely used to refer to the energy produced by radioactivity.

radioactivity Property of some naturally occuring and synthetic substances to spontaneously emit energy which is harmful to life in anything but very small doses.

radioisotope Radioactive form of an element; carbon-14 is a radioisotope of carbon.

rain forest Extremely lush and diverse form of natural vegetation that occurs mainly in tropical regions. The tropical rain forests contain at least half of all species on Earth, and are also vital to the proper functioning of the atmosphere.

ranching Raising beef cattle on large areas of grassland. Ranching was developed in Spain, and was then exported to North and South America, and later to Australasia.

secondary consumers Meat eaters (carnivores). They are called secondary consumers because the energy they receive from food has already been processed by primary consumers (herbivores).

seine Long net that is drawn around a school of fish and closed like a purse.

selective breeding Technique for improving the quality of crops or livestock. Only individuals with desirable characteristics are chosen to reproduce for the next generation.

sisal Material made from the fibers of one of the most widely cultivated plants of the agave family.

slash-and-burn Type of primitive agriculture now confined to tropical rain forests. It gets its name from the method used to clear vegetation. The ash fertilizes the soil, but a piece of land can be used only once every 30 years.

sleeping sickness Disease spread by insect bites that afflicts both humans and animals over large areas of central Africa.

smog Form of localized atmospheric pollution that occurs over some large cities. The action of sunlight on vehicle exhaust fumes creates a thick layer of dirty and often poisonous air.

soil erosion Loss of topsoil (the most fertile layer) through the action of wind and water.

species The most precise form of grouping of a type of plant or animal. All members of the same species have the same characteristics and differ only slightly in size or markings. Breeding generally does not take place between different species.

staple Any crop that forms the basis of the daily diet in a particular region. Most staples are cereals, but vegetables such as potatoes and cassava are often grown as staple crops.

subsistence Describes any form of agriculture where all the produce is used to support the farmer and the farmer's family.

succession Process by which an area of new or cleared ground is occupied by a series of species. Fast-growing plants with windborne seeds are usually the first species to establish themselves.

trawl Bag-shaped net pulled behind a boat. Trawling is the main method of catching demersal fish.

understory Layer of relatively open space that occurs inside rain forests, between the forest floor and the dense foliage of the treetops (the canopy).

zooplankton Minute aquatic animals, food for the smallest of the underwater predators.

Index

Page numbers in *italics* refer to pictures. Users of this Index should note that explanations of many scientific terms can be found in the glossary.

P

paddy fields *54*, 56, 76, 85
Panama 27
papaya *58*
parasites 36, 72
passenger pigeon 30
passion fruit *58*
pelagic fish 80
perch *13*
permafrost 20, 24
persimmon *58*
Peru 79
pesticides 27, 39, 48, 52, 57, 72
pests 36-37
pets 28, 29, 32
Philippines 52, 54
photosynthesis 10, 12, 23, 54, 79
phytoplankton *13*, *16*, 17, 79
pigeons 37
pigs 52, 70, 71
pineapple *58*
plaice 80
plankton 8, 17
plantations 22, 58, 62
plow 50
poachers 34, 35
polar bears 36
pollen 14
pollution 38-45, 47, 80
   air 40-41
    water 44-45
pomegranate *58*
Portugal 78
potato 52, 54, 58
poultry 70, 76-77
prairie 20, 29
predators 12, 17
primates 32
Przewalski's horse *34*

R

rabbits 64
racoons 36
rain forest 8, 14-15, 18
   destruction of 22-23
rainfall 21, 23
rambutan *58*
ramie 62
rape *61*
rats 36, *36*
red stainer bug *14*
Rhine River 44
rhino 34
rice 49, 52, 54, 55, 56, *56*,
   57
rye 52, 56, *56*

S

Saanen goat *75*
Sahara Desert 21
salmon 80, 85
Santa Gertrudis cattle *53*
sapodilla *58*
sardines 80, *82*
sea cucumber *17*
sea gulls 37
seine fishing 83
selective breeding
   in dairy cattle 66
   in farm animals 52-53
shark *16*, 17
sheep 49, 52, 70, 72, 73
shelduck *11*
shellfish 78
shepherd's purse 37
shorthorn cattle *53*, 65, 66
Siberia 24
Simmental cattle *68*
sisal 62
skate *17*
slash-and-burn agriculture 50, *50*
small white butterfly *37*
smog *41*
Soay sheep 72
soil erosion 18
sorghum *50*
soursop *58*
South Africa 72
South America 14, 22, 68
southern right whale *32-33*
Soviet Union 25, 43, 60, 62, 78, 80
soybeans 51
Spain 65
squid *17*
Sri Lanka 63
staple crops 54
stickleback *13*
stilt *11*
subsistence agriculture 50
   cattle herding in 65
   fruit in 58
succession 11
Sudan 25
Sudanese sheep 72
sugar 60, *60*
sulfur dioxide 38, 41
Switzerland 74

T

tea 62, 63
thick-lipped gray mullet *84*
tigers 35
timber 19, 27

Toulouse geese *77*
trawling *78*
tripod fish *17*
triticale *52*
trophic levels 12
tropical rain forest *see rain forest*
trout 85
tuna 80
Turkey 74
turkeys 76

U

United States 20, 23, *27*, 28, 29, 38,
   42, 43, 48, 53, 59, 60, 61, 62, 64,
   65, 82
   fish farming in 84, *85*
   poultry farming in 70, 76
uranium 24

V

veal 68
vegetables 59
vitamins 58

W

water beetle *13*
water buffalo 56
weed killers 55
Welsh Black cattle *69*
West African dwarf sheep *72*
wetlands 27
whales 17, 32
wheat *47*, 49, 52, 54, 56, *56*, *57*
white rhinoceros *35*
Wicken Fen, England *26*
winged bean 59
woodland 9, 11, 27
wool 72
World Wildlife Fund (WWF) 34, 35

Y

yeheb bush 59
Yellowstone National Park 27

Z

Zambesi River *25*
zebra *29*
zebu cattle 53, 54, 65, 68
zooplankton *13*, *16*, 17

Further reading

Banks, Martin. *Endangered Wildlife*. Vero Beach, Fla.: Rourke, 1988.

Bowman, Keith. *Agriculture*. Morristown, N.J.: Silver Burdett, 1987.

Bramwell, Martyn. *Oceanography*. New York: Hampstead Press/Watts, 1989.

Burton, John. *Close to Extinction*. New York: Gloucester Press/Watts, 1988.

Curtis, Patricia. *All Creatures Welcome: The Story of a Wildlife Rehabilitation Center*. New York: Lodestar Books/Dutton, 1985.

Donnelly, Judy, and Sydelle Kramer. *Space Junk: Pollution Beyond the Earth*. New York: Morrow, 1990.

Fine, John Christopher. *The Hunger Road*. New York: Atheneum/Macmillan, 1988.

Gay, Kathlyn. *Silent Killers: Radon and Other Hazards*. New York: Franklin Watts, 1988.

Giblin, James Cross. *Milk: The Fight for Purity*. New York: Thomas Y. Crowell/Harper, 1986.

Gorman, Carol. *America's Farm Crisis*. New York: Franklin Watts, 1987.

Lambert, David. *Planet Earth 2000*. New York: Facts on File, 1986.

Markham, Adam. *The Environment*. Vero Beach, Fla.: Rourke, 1988.

McCormick, John. *Acid Rain*. New York: Gloucester Press/Watts, 1986.

Miller, Christina G., and Louise A. Berry. *Acid Rain: A Sourcebook for Young People*. New York: Messner, 1986.

Miller, Christina G., and Louise A. Berry. *Coastal Rescue: Preserving Our Seashores*. New York: Atheneum/Macmillan, 1989.

Milne, Lorus J., and Margery Milne. *A Shovelful of Earth*. New York: Holt, 1987.

Nations, James D. *Tropical Rainforests: Endangered Environments*. New York: Franklin Watts, 1988.

Pringle, Laurence P. *Saving our Wildlife*. Hillside, N.J.: Enslow Publishers, 1990.

Sagan, Dorion, and Lynn Margulis. *Biospheres From Earth to Space*. Hillside, N.J.: Enslow Publishers, 1989.

Sedge, Michael H. *Commercialization of the Oceans*. New York: Franklin Watts, 1987.

Simon, Noel. *Vanishing Habitats*. New York: Gloucester Press/Watts, 1987.

Smith, Howard E., Jr. *Small Worlds: Communities of Living Things*. New York: Scribner, 1987.

Picture Credits

b=bottom, t=top, l=left, c=center, r=right.
ANT Australasian Nature Transparencies. BCL
Bruce Coleman Ltd. London. HL Hutchison
Library, London. NHPA Natural History
Photographic Agency, Ardingly, Sussex. OSF
Oxford Scientific Films, Long Hanborough,
Oxfordshire. PEP Planet Earth Pictures, London.
RHPL Robert Harding Picture Library, London.
SPL Science Photo Library, London.

6 Zefa/K. Benser. 8 NHPA/David Woodfall. 10t
Premaphotos Wildlife. 10b PEP/J. Scott. 11
Anthony Bannister. 14c NHPA/Harold Palo Jr. 14b
Michael Fogden. 15tr Biofotos/Soames
Summerhays. 15cl OSF/D.Thompson. 15br
NHPA/Harold Palo Jr. 16 PEP/Peter David. 17
PEP/Herwarth Voigtmann. 18 HL/Richard House.
19 HL/Patricio Goycolea. 20 Zefa/B. Crader. 22
SPL/Earth Satellite Corporation. 22-23 ANT. 23
RHPL/John G. Ross. 24 BCL/David Davies. 25t A.
Charnock. 25b Peter Fraenkel. 26t NHPA/David
Woodfall. 26b Zefa. 26-27b Doug Weschler. 28 OSF/
Rob Cousins. 29r OSF. 29l Aspect/Tom Nebbia.
32-33 BCL/Francisco Erize. 33l RHPL. 33r Peter
Veit. 34t Biofotos/Heather Angel. 34b NHPA/
Douglas Dickins. 35t George Frame. 35bl PEP/
Arup & Marioj Shah. 35br Ardea. 38 Survival
Anglia/Jeff Foott. 39l Zefa. 39r, 40 Rex Features.
40-41 South American Pictures/Tony Morrison. 41
Biofotos/Heather Angel. 42 Colorific/Bill Pierce. 43l
Novosti Press Agency. 43r Frank Spooner/Gamma.
44t, 45 Susan Griggs Agency/Martin Rogers. 44b
Zefa. 46 Zefa/M. Thonig. 48 Telegraph Color
Library/Alex Low. 49 Ronald Sheridan/Ancient Art
& Architecture Collection. 50t Zefa. 50b BCL/L. C.
Marigo. 51 Zefa. 52 Holt Studios. 53 Art Directors/
Chuck O'Rear. 54 ANT/Gordon Claridge. 57l
NHPA/N. A. Callow. 57r John & Penny Hubley.
57b BCL/Nicholas De Vore. 60l, 60r HL. 61t HL/
John Downman. 61b Premaphotos Wildlife/K. G.
Preston-Mafham. 62 HL/Dave Brincombe. 63l HL/
Sarah Errington Pollock. 63r HL/Timothy Beddow.
64 HL/S. Porlock. 65 RHPL/G. S. Corrigan. 69
Aquila/M. & V. Lane. 70 HL. 73 Ardea/J. P.
Ferrero. 73 (inset) Swift Picture Library/R.
Fletcher. 74l A. Mowlem. 74r BCL. 76t BCL/
Cameron Davidson. 76b RHPL. 77t BCL/B. D.
Hamilton. 77b Agence Nature/J. P. Ferrero. 78
PEP/J. Duncan. 79 NHPA/Peter Johnson. 81, 82
RHPL. 84l PEP/J. & G. Lythgoe. 84r BCL/D.
Goulston. 85 BCL/K. Gunnar.